Praise for

Treat Me Like a Customer

Recently, I vowed to be more intentional, particularly with respect to my relationships and interactions with family. Louis's message in this book might serve as an epiphany for others to reach a similar conclusion.

> —John Ingram, Chairman, Ingram Industries Inc.

In my career in branding and marketing, I've always felt the most impactful and powerful ideas are generated from seemingly simple concepts. In this book, Louis Upkins has—with laserlike effectiveness—found such a concept.

> —Lou Weisbach, CEO, Stadium Capital Financing Group

Wow! Definitely a home run. It is critical to find the proper balance in one's life, and this book contains keys and best practices.

> —C. Kemmons Wilson Jr., Chairman, Wilson Hotel
> Management Company

Louis Upkins' book is timely and relevant in today's fast-paced business environment. Louis's ability to apply certain customer-service principles to how we treat our families is extremely insightful. I encourage all professionals to read this book and bring balance back into their lives.

> —Stuart McWhorter, Cofounder and President,
> Clayton Associates

Louis Upkins' book has such a simple premise: you will have a better marriage and family by treating your wife and kids as if they were your customers. Sound strange? It's actually very smart, and I urge you to read this book. It's chock-full of wisdom and insights.

—BILL MILLIKEN, Founder and Vice Chair, Communities in Schools; author, *The Last Dropout: Stop the Epidemic*

In this book, Louis Upkins clearly and succinctly reminds us what our priorities should be. He identifies simple tools that can be used to strengthen our marriages and our families, which will, in turn, provide all of us with the balance we need to continue to be successful in our careers. As a successful female executive in corporate America, I find that what Louis is discussing is my reality. His words have inspired me to ensure that my most precious gifts (my husband and sons) are treated like my customers. This book is both powerful and life changing!

—SONIA JACKSON MYLES, Fortune 500 top-level executive; author, *The Sister Accord*

While I am not expert on being successful in marriage, perhaps I would have been if I had had the opportunity to read this book when I was a young bride. As the mom of the thirty-five-thousand-member Southwest Airlines family, I did (and do) subscribe to Louis Upkins' philosophies concerning proactive customer-service delivery with no distinction in terms of importance between internal and external customers. I credit this egalitarian spirit as the principal ingredient of our successful family culture.

—COLLEEN BARRETT, President Emeritus, Southwest Airlines

TREAT *me* LIKE A CUSTOMER

Using Lessons from Work to Succeed in Life

LOUIS UPKINS

ZONDERVAN®

ZONDERVAN.com/
AUTHORTRACKER
follow your favorite authors

ZONDERVAN

Treat Me Like a Customer
Copyright © 2009 by Louis Upkins

This title is also available as a Zondervan ebook. Visit www.zondervan.com/ebooks.

This title is also available in a Zondervan audio edition. Visit www.zondervan.fm.

Requests for information should be addressed to:
Zondervan, *Grand Rapids, Michigan* 49530

Library of Congress Cataloging-in-Publication Data

Upkins, Louis, 1963–
    Treat me like a customer : using lessons from work to succeed in life /
Louis Upkins.
        p.   cm.
    Includes bibliographical references.
    ISBN 978-0-310-32029-6 (hardcover, jacketed)
    1. Success. 2. Marriage. 3. Success in business. I. Title.
BJ1611.2.U65   2009
158.2—dc22   2009026827

Any Internet addresses (websites, blogs, etc.) and telephone numbers printed in this book are offered as a resource. They are not intended in any way to be or imply an endorsement by Zondervan, nor does Zondervan vouch for the content of these sites and numbers for the life of this book.

Published in association with Rosenbaum & Associates Literary Agency, Brentwood, Tennessee.

Interior design by Beth Shagene

Printed in the United States of America

---

09 10 11 12 13 14 15 • 23 22 21 20 19 18 17 16 15 14 13 12 11 10 9 8 7 6 5 4 3 2 1

To my wife, Charita,
and our children, Caleb and Zoé

Contents

Foreword

WHEN I WAS THIRTY-FOUR YEARS OLD, I WAS GIVEN THE responsibility of running my family's cable television business. Confident that with a lot of hard work I could successfully grow the business, I was less sure of what running a business would do to other areas of my life. A question tugged at a corner of my mind: "What might you lose with all this gaining?" I had seen how success had robbed others of their marriages, families, health, and values and did not want that to happen to me. So I thought about what I wanted to accomplish most and described that with six goals. Several years later, when I entered what I call "halftime" and started Leadership Network, I developed another list—seven commitments to help me stay focused on my life mission.

You can see these lists in my book *Halftime*, but one commitment that appears on both bears mentioning here: to have a vital marriage to my wife, Linda, until "death do us part." By putting my marriage on the same level as my career goals—first with my career in television and then with my "second half" career with Leadership Network—I was ensuring that it would receive the attention it deserved. It has, and with God's grace and Linda's patience, we are still married.

Trust me, I thank God every morning for such a solid marriage that is approaching its fiftieth year. I am fully aware of the failure rate of American marriages and sadly accept the fact that it's not much better in the church. I also know that a good share of those marriages that remain intact struggle to maintain their vitality. Which is why I was so intrigued with Louis Upkins' idea for a book when he first shared it with me. Having spent most of my career in business, I can relate to his premise. In our work, we will do just about anything to please our customers, but at home we somehow forget all those skills to the detriment of our marriages. Louis believes, and I tend to agree, that you don't really have to learn new skills or even work that hard to improve the quality of your marriage. If you just begin treating your spouse the way you treat your customers, clients, and colleagues at work, the results will be astounding.

In *Treat Me Like a Customer*, Louis reminds us of the skills we all use at work to grow our businesses and then shows us how to use them at home. Highly practical and refreshingly down to earth, he writes as a fellow traveler rather than a professional counselor. I have learned over the years that men have a hard time talking to each other about their marriages, especially if their marriages are experiencing difficulties. Reading this book is like sitting down with a close friend and having that honest conversation.

—Bob Buford, author of *Halftime*

Preface

ALL OF US HAVE CUSTOMERS. AS A BUSINESSMAN, THE PEOPLE I work with daily and have the privilege of serving are my customers. If you are a lawyer, you represent your customers in their legal matters. If you build things or repair things, your customers expect you to perform miracles with tools. If you are a schoolteacher, your customers are your students and their parents, and they are not always easy to please. But you try hard every day.

Many of us have another type of customer: a supervisor, a board, or another authority we report to. They are like customers because we depend on them for our jobs and therefore do our best to deliver the results they expect. And in some ways, our colleagues and coworkers are like customers because we want to get along with them and help them become successful.

Our customers keep us in business, so of course we want to satisfy them. Whenever we are with them, we put on our best faces and show them how much they matter to us. When they ask us to do something, we get right on it. They become our top priority. Under-promise, overdeliver — isn't that our mantra? We want them to be impressed with our work, not so much for our sakes but for theirs. Few things are as satisfying as successfully meeting the needs of a customer, knowing that the product or service we provided made them more successful.

Sometimes our customers are difficult and unreasonable, but we treat them as if they are the most important people on earth. Sometimes they are hard to please, but we respond with patience and perseverance. Even if a customer does something to upset us, we try not to show it.

In this book, I will show you how you will have a better marriage and family by treating your wife and kids as if they were your customers. I know—sounds a little strange. Maybe even insulting. Your wife and kids are *so* much more important to you than your customers, right? Of course they are, but do *they* know that, and do you show that? Do you go out of your way to please them like you do your colleagues and customers at work?

The title for this book quotes the wife of a friend of mine. This couple wasn't on their way to divorce court, but like a lot of marriages, theirs was not as great as it could be, not as fulfilling as they both wanted it to be. Her heartfelt plea made a lot of sense to me. Maybe the advice we need for better marriages is right under our noses. Maybe turning good marriages into great marriages is easier than we think.

I have written this book with men in mind, primarily because in my opinion women who work outside the home seem to be doing a better job of balancing work and family than men. That could be changing as more and more women find themselves in demanding professions. I have consulted with a few businesswomen about the premise of this book, and they feel that it could easily apply to their lives. So if you bought this book for your husband and both of you lead busy lives in the marketplace, you may find it helpful to you as well.

As you continue reading, you will notice that most of my examples come from people in leadership or management positions. That doesn't mean the principles in this book don't apply to you if you are a carpenter or a schoolteacher; it's just a reflection of my particular world. I'm confident that regardless of your profession, if you put the skills I discuss in this book to work in your marriage—just as you do at work—you will have a stronger, more fulfilling relationship with your spouse.

I love my wife and children, but I want to do better. I know you love yours too and desire to keep those relationships strong and healthy. Together, in this book, we will learn how to transform our marriages (and with them, our families) by using the skills that make us so successful at work.

Acknowledgments

When the concept of this book was birthed, I knew it would take a lot of help from people a lot smarter than me to accomplish this task. I am thankful for the way my family—Charita, Caleb, and Zoé—let me tuck away in different parts of the house as well as at Starbucks to write and then read my thoughts out loud. Their patience and support made it easy.

I also have to give credit to Bob Buford, who in his unique way supported me by asking questions and opening doors. Without his direction, this book would not have been possible. Lyn Cryderman was a great partner to help me shape my thoughts and articulate my heart. Kemmons and Norma Wilson provided a living example of what balance combined with success looks like. Steven Burgess recognized this burden in my heart a year ago and encouraged me to write about it. I can't say enough about Stuart and Leigh Anne McWhorter's support and friendship. They are the best of friends! Simon Bailey sent me every article known to man on how to write a book and showed unselfish support. Lou Weisbach never ceases to amaze me. Marty Dickens, Bill Lee, Sam Bartholomew, Stedman Graham, Dave Steward, and Jim Caden—I thank each of them for their wisdom. Israel Houghton stood by me through the process and

I thank him for that. Bucky Rosenbaum expertly guided me through the ups and downs of getting a book published. And finally, I thank the entire Zondervan family for their work on this project.

This book was inspired by all the good and the bad I have seen in businesses and families around the world. My prayer is that it will unleash hope, responsibility, and permission for families to honor and cherish the gift of love. I hope that you find yourself somewhere in the things you underline in this book and use those points to shape and direct you toward a life of purpose, balance, and wonderful times with your family.

Let's go have some fun!

Learning
on the Job

WHEN I STARTED MY CAREER AS AN ENTREPRENEUR, WRITING A book like this was the last thing I thought I would ever do. I was still in college, working on an engineering degree, when a local businesswoman asked me to design a T-shirt for her business. Apparently the design I came up with was successful, because she sold a ton of them and asked me to design some more. Even though I was still a student carrying a full load of classes, I took all the work she could give me because I needed the money. When I noticed how well the T-shirts with my designs sold, I decided to do a little research about how to make T-shirts and eventually started my own little design business. My engineering degree seemed like the right thing for me to do, but my heart was in design. Over the next several years, two things happened. First, my business grew. I mean it really grew. Not without a lot of hard work and the occasional setback that comes with running your own business, but I have served clients such as Starbucks, Burger King, and Oprah Winfrey, to name a few.

But in recent years, something else has begun to happen. As I developed long-term relationships with some of my clients — highly successful CEOs, entrepreneurs, and business leaders — they started talking to me about their lives. I don't mean just their hobbies or their personal interests; that sort of thing is common among men. These guys were opening up to me about their marriages, their children, their beliefs, their frustrations, and their fears. I was taken aback at first. For obvious reasons, I thought that these guys had it all—wealth, freedom, success, accomplishment. They generally were well respected in their communities and active in philanthropic endeavors that often brought them recognition and admiration. And yet once they opened up to me, it was clear they weren't very happy. In fact, they were anything *but* happy.

I remember one day when I got a call from a friend—I'll call him Michael—who is a successful executive who has built his business by inspiring others with his great vision and ability, and whom I respect for what he does for others. I nonchalantly asked him how his day was going, and he blew my mind when he responded, "Louis, my professional life is great, but my personal life is hell."

Wow! Here is a guy who really has experienced the American Dream, but as far as he's concerned it has become a nightmare. Like so many men, he did all the right things. Married, went to work to provide for his growing family, built a successful business that provides jobs for others, got involved in his community, and kept active in his church. By all accounts, at this stage in his life he should be enjoying the fruit of all his hard work, but he's miserable. As we talked, he let the title of a 2007 Tyler Perry blockbuster movie speak his thoughts: *Why Did I Get Married?* I could hardly believe my ears. What I thought was just a casual conversation with a friend turned into a confession that he was thinking about walking away from everything he had worked so hard to support.

If my conversation with Michael had been an isolated incident, I guess I would just conclude that he made a few mistakes and was frustrated and leave it at that. But this sort of thing happens to me almost every week; successful business leaders and other professionals open up to me and many of them share the same story: "Things couldn't be better at work, but my personal life is a mess." And believe me, this doesn't happen just with people I know. Many times I'll get a call from a perfect stranger and he'll start the conversation with something like, "Michael told me I should give you a call."

For whatever reason, I've become something of a confessional mentor to a lot of men from all walks of life. Just a few days before writing this, I was speaking to a small group of eighty CEOs and business executives about balance and life as a CEO at an event sponsored by a major national bank. At the conclusion of the event, at least seventy of them lined up to speak with me, many admitting to their own personal struggles. It was affirming, but it was also a little sad to realize that so much of what we see on the outside of a person does not always represent what's going on inside. On a recent business trip, when I was flying home from Southern California, I grabbed a copy of *Fortune* magazine and noted it contained their Fortune 400 Rich List. So I eagerly turned to the list and started reading the profiles of these extremely successful business leaders. One glaring statistic caught my attention: more than one hundred of the four hundred men had been divorced more than once! Stories like that confirm what I am learning from the men who come to me for help: success at work has little to do with success in life.

I am not really sure why men come to me except that they see I'm still married to the same woman I fell in love with when I was a young man and they know they can trust me. To be perfectly candid, the odds of staying married were against us. While I have been blessed with great parents, they divorced when I was sixteen. And my wife, Charita, also experienced the divorce of her parents. Most marriage experts report that children of divorce are more likely to be divorced themselves, so why have Charita and I been able not just to stay married for almost thirteen years but actually to enjoy being married and look forward to spending the rest of our lives together? As faithful followers of Christ, we both credit God for blessing our marriage and strengthening our love for each other, but many of the men who share their problems with me are similarly devoted to trusting God. As we all have so painfully realized, being a Christian does not guarantee that our lives work out the way we would like them to. The divorce rate in the church is very close to the divorce rate outside the church. So while I credit God for protecting our marriage, I know he has used other things to keep our love for each other so strong. Like my paying attention to what happened to my family as I was growing up.

Success at Work *and* at Home

My parents came from humble beginnings, and my dad did a great job providing for us. For an African-American man living in the South, the only work available that paid a halfway decent wage was construction, and my dad worked hard and well with his hands. But I'll never forget the day he came home and announced he was quitting his job to start his own construction company. I was so proud of him! I can remember it like it was yesterday—the entire family sitting at the dinner table and listening to my father tell the story with courage and determination of what pushed him to work for himself.

I remember it well because it marked the beginning of a new chapter for us. As he put in long hours to build a very successful company, we saw less and less of him. I don't really blame him, because I knew he thought he was doing the right thing. Our standard of living improved, and I knew all of his hard work was done for us, but it was clear he had to focus on this new company, and sometimes that brought both good and bad times.

His company came first, therefore my mother filled in for him, spending most of her time with us and the sports and hobbies we enjoyed. It didn't help that when we got out of control my mother would tell us, "Just wait until your father gets home." What boy wants to see his daddy if all he's going to get is a spanking? But of course, every boy wants to see his daddy — to sit in his lap and listen to stories, or to throw a football to him in the back yard. Every boy wants to see his daddy come home and kiss his mommy and sit down for a nice family dinner. Unfortunately, we don't always get what we want, and eventually my parents ended their marriage.

During those early years, however, I too had my priorities out of order in that I really had no room for God in my busy life. Growing up, I really didn't know God for myself. I knew very little of what it means to be a man and even less about what it means to be a man of God. Thankfully, through the prayers of others and a dynamic church, I surrendered my life to Christ while I was still a young man. Once I got my life in balance, I resolved to keep it that way. I wanted to make sure that nothing became more important to me than my relationship with God.

In terms of my earthly relationships, Charita would come first. If we had children, I would be active in their lives, and I would seek out relationships with other godly men to hold me accountable. And through God's grace, that's exactly what I have been able to do. We don't have a perfect marriage. (Is there really such a thing?) But I can honestly say Charita is my best friend, and at the risk of sounding arrogant, whenever I have had to choose between an important business meeting or trip and an important family event, about 98 percent of the time I have chosen family.

Despite the challenges of running a company, I try to set aside some time each day to listen to my kids, giving them my full attention. And I have been blessed with some very good friends who meet with me, pray with me, hold me accountable, and give me encouragement when I need it. I saw what didn't work in my own family and decided early on that I wouldn't make the same mistakes.

But it doesn't just happen. I have had to be intentional about all of this because in the world we all live in, this huge gravitational pull tries to separate us from what we consider to be most important to us. Ironically, it's often the good things that get in the way: church, school, civic responsibilities.

Think about it. If you ask anyone what's most important to him, he'll tell you it's his family. As we wait for a connecting flight in an airport, we pull out pictures of our children and tell stories about soccer games and spelling bees. And I truly believe that on the surface at least—or in our intentions—we all highly value our wives and children. I've yet to hear a man tell me he hates his wife and wants to get as far away from his children as possible. Sadly, many people who truly love each other are contributing to the 60 percent divorce rate in America.

I recall talking to a guy who was in such turmoil over his marriage. "I think I'll just move out and get my own apartment," he said after earlier acknowledging that he still loved his wife. He just felt it would be too hard to repair their relationship, and like so many men, he felt the best way to handle his problems was to try to escape them. I urged him to hang in there and work things out, because I knew his solution was a cop-out and that it not only would hurt her but later would hurt him as well. I reminded him what the Bible teaches about difficulties in marriage: for better or for worse. "Today may feel like the worst for you," I concluded. "But leaving is not an option."

Good advice, but just telling someone to hang in there doesn't always work, and that is why I am writing this book. Even if you believe you have a pretty good marriage, you can't just leave it on autopilot and hope for the best. When you don't pay attention to details at work, things go south pretty fast, and the same thing happens in marriages. That's why we are usually shocked to learn that a couple we know pretty well is headed for divorce court; they seemed to really love each other, and probably did, but drifted apart because they made other things more important than their marriage. Unfortunately, difficult marriages hurt more than the couples involved.

Regardless of what the experts may say about our nation's major problems, like crime, drugs, underperforming schools, and poverty, I believe deteriorating families lead to a deteriorating society. Problems at home become problems in our culture. It has become almost abnormal to pay attention to what matters most. Some of the most successful people I know have unbelievably messed up personal lives yet continue to pour themselves into their careers as if they believe making more money will solve all of their problems. Your marriage may not be in trouble. You may feel it's going pretty well. My caution to you is not to become complacent or make the mistake of thinking a lack of conflict means that everything is great. I truly believe it's possible to be a success at work *and* at home, but we have to invest ourselves in both venues.

As I mentioned earlier, the idea for this book came from one of those guys who was a success at work, a friend of mine who fits the profile of success: great career, dedicated wife, lovely children, comfortable home in a desirable neighborhood. He and I were discussing what I should be doing instead of designing T-shirts and creating branding plans for major companies. It was like he was sent to encourage me on a day when I really needed a boost.

"Louis," he said, "what you should be doing full time is speaking into the lives of men like me every day because you have an ability to see into the depths of the heart and see the traps we fall into and then love us out of them."

I was taken aback, but he really caught my attention when he offered to hire me to help him develop his "life plan." From everything I knew about him, I assumed he not only had a pretty good plan but was well on his way to executing it superbly.

"The truth is, Louis, we're just making it up as we go along," he replied when I expressed surprise at his request. "In fact, I'm going to call my wife right now and ask about our life plan," and the next thing I knew he had dialed his wife and put her on the speakerphone.

"Honey, can you remind me what our life plan is?" he asked into the phone.

"Harold, the only plan we have is this: you run the business and I run the house, and you don't have a clue what I do or need," she replied, and Harold gave me a look laced with resignation.

Later, he told me that when he got home that night, his wife seemed a little annoyed at his phone call. He was tired and wanted to get comfortable, so he gave her all the signals that he wanted to be left alone. That's when she greeted him with these words: "Harold, just suck it up and treat me like one of your customers."

Ouch!

But that thought was a revelation to me. On the surface, it may seem simplistic or even offensive. Of *course* our families and close friends are far more valuable than any customer. To even to think of them as customers seems demeaning. Yet the more I thought about it, the more I came to believe that this simple request from Harold's wife holds the key for returning some balance to our lives. Without realizing it, many men have allowed their valued customers and people who affect the bottom line to supplant the people who are closest to them. If a valued customer calls and wants a meeting, we drop everything and rearrange our schedules to accommodate him. When we get to the meeting, we make sure everything is just right to make him comfortable. We show him respect by putting a welcome sign in the entrance of our building with his name on it. We escort him to a well-appointed conference room and have his coffee ready for him just as he likes it. We have our best presentation ready and listen carefully to his questions. And before he arrives back in his office, we already have an email waiting for him, thanking him for his time.

Contrast that with what happens when your wife asks if she could meet you for lunch someday.

"Oh, I'd love to, honey, but I have some huge deadlines today."

"I promised Ben I'd go over sales figures with him over lunch."

"We just did that last week."

Then think about all of the football games, school plays, concerts, field trips, and sleepovers you've missed because you were out of town on business. Think of the times you had good intentions to meet with a group of men to pray for and support each other, but you had too much on your plate at work. I *know* all of those activities are more important to you than your work, but your life is so out of balance that by necessity they have had to take second place. The customer comes first, and your family and friends aren't customers.

Well, what would happen if you treated the people who are most important to you the same way you treat a valued customer? It won't necessarily be easy to do this, but you do not have to learn anything new, and it will be well worth the effort. I will show you how you can apply all the great skills you use every day building a successful career to have a successful personal life. I will share stories from some of today's most successful leaders who have practiced this concept without missing a beat in their careers. People like Dave Steward, the successful head of Worldwide Technology, a nationally recognized company, who stunned me when he said if he has to choose between his family and a work-related function, his family always wins. Always! I thought at the time that if he can do that and be a successful leader, anyone can. He runs a multi-billion-dollar company!

Live Like There's No Tomorrow

Several weeks ago I was driving my son, Caleb, to school, enjoying this brief time we have together every morning. I had made it a policy always to shut my cell phone off during these times, and on this day I was so glad I did because Caleb was filled with stories he wanted to tell me. It was such a sweet experience that I didn't want it to end. As I pulled into the school's parking lot, I saw Caleb's teacher and she was rubbing her eyes, so I decided to have a little fun with her.

"Wake up, Ms. Blue," I shouted out the window, and then I regretted my levity when I saw that she had been crying.

I learned that on the very road I travel to bring Caleb to school every day, another teacher from his school had been killed in an automobile accident the night before. He too had a young family, and I couldn't help but think how quickly our lives can end and how taking the time to listen to my son may have been the most important thing I did that day. I thought back on the many men who shared with me their sorrow at pouring themselves into their careers at the expense of their families and wondered how they might change their priorities if they knew they would die tomorrow.

I am convinced that you desire to keep your priorities in order and want to regain some balance in your life, that you want nothing more than to live the life God intends for you to live. But if the hundreds of men who come to me are any indication, I also believe you are wrestling with guilt and regret over the way things have turned out for you. You may feel like giving up, or at least plodding along on autopilot, resigned to accept things the way they are.

If this describes you, hang in there! It *can* be better, and you already have all the tools to make it happen. It will take some hard work on your part, but then all good things require a little effort. This approach to improving your marriage won't cost a dime, and within a very short time you will begin to see positive results. Not only will your wife and children and closest friends immediately recognize a difference, but your colleagues at work will be just as favorably impressed. With a little practice, it will become a lifestyle, one that you always imagined. And here's the best news: you really don't have to learn anything new. You can regain balance in your life and enjoy the blessings of your closest relationships by doing with your family what you already do so well at work: giving your customers and colleagues the respect and priority they deserve.

2

Why You're Having Such a Hard Time

W HO WOULD HAVE THOUGHT THAT A FIRST-CLASS SEAT ON A flight to Paris could feel like such a prison? But for Derrick, the offer of a drink from the friendly flight attendant and the prospect of a nice meal served on fine china later in the flight did little to lift his spirits. Even knowing that when he landed in Paris a driver would take him to the spectacular La Tremoille hotel couldn't ease the misery he felt deep in his soul. A dynamic leader with a great track record at his company, Derrick was never prone to self-pity. When faced with a daunting challenge at work, he loved the adrenaline rush that took over and the satisfaction that came in solving yet another problem. But as the plane was pushed out onto the tarmac and he saw the familiar sight of his hometown airport disappearing from view, it became a metaphor for his life: everything he really cared about was gradually slipping away.

I run into a lot of men like Derrick. Good men. Successful men. Men who go to work every day to provide for their families and coach Little League teams and go to dance recitals. Men who seem to have their priorities straight and have invested heavily into their families. CEOs and construction workers. Lawyers and laborers. Engineers and educators. They may not share the same net worth or wear the same uniform to work, but they do have one thing in common: like Derrick, they feel as if they are drifting farther and farther away from the people who matter most to them, and they don't like it. It's not that they're heading for divorce court or that their marriages are seriously troubled. As marriages go, theirs are not bad. But not bad isn't good enough. And what makes it all the harder for them is that on the surface, it doesn't seem fair.

"Hey," one of these men raised his voice out of frustration and almost shouted to me over breakfast in a restaurant. "I'm doing all the right things, but all I get at home is grief!"

In a way, I had to agree with his perception of things. I knew him to be a man who was doing his best to balance the demands of his job with his devotion to his family. These guys aren't out all night chasing other women. Or wasting all their money at the casino. They aren't heavy drinkers or insensitive slobs who just want to be left alone in front of the television. These are honest, hardworking men who try to leave work early to catch a soccer game and who always stop at the airport gift shop on the way home from a business trip, even if it is an afterthought. If you could peek into their living rooms on Christmas morning, you would see happy kids and an adoring wife — the picture of domestic bliss. But these are the same guys who tell me that they feel like strangers to their wives or that their kids have been busted for underage drinking. They're frustrated because they believe all their hard work to provide for their families should be making things better for everyone.

Sound familiar?

Why are we having such a hard time balancing work with the people and activities we love the most? How can so many decent, churchgoing, family-values supporting, productive citizens struggle with what they believe to be the very fabric of society: marriage and family?

Doing the Right Things

If you're like most of the men I've met, you are probably doing all the right things. I mean, what are we generally taught by both church and society? Try to better yourself. Go to college. Find a career that puts your skills and knowledge to work. Earn enough money to provide for your family and establish financial security. Buy a house. Set aside money for your kids' education. Give back to the community by volunteering for good causes and supporting your church financially. And if you're like me, you'd like to give your kids some of the things you never had when you were a kid. Not spoil them, but not deprive them either.

How could all of these right things cause so much grief for you and your family?

Trust me, most of the men I know would get an A+ in all of these categories. Yet many of them are struggling with balance, just as I suspect you might be also, so let's take a closer look at what really happens during that brief time between when we say "I do" and when we discover something's wrong—a span of about ten to fifteen years for most of us.

I learned early in life that if you want to get ahead, you have to work. Success, no matter how you define it, doesn't come easily. Most of us developed a solid work ethic in college. We worked long hours on summer jobs to save up for the coming school year. Many of us not only went to class and stayed up late doing our homework but held down part-time jobs as well. Sure, it wasn't easy, but it was what we did, what it took to become successful.

Along the way, we met the love of our lives. Do you remember that instant when you fell head over heels and knew you had found the woman you wanted to be with for the rest of your life? If you're like me, you would have done anything for her. Even though you were on a Steak and Shake budget, you'd work extra hours to be able

to take her to a five-star restaurant (and that should have been a clue).
Nothing was too good for her when it came to gifts, and no matter
what it took, you would show up with something special you bought
to show her how much she meant to you.

I'll never forget the first time Charita let me come over to her
place. She had been really sick and hadn't eaten for a couple of days

Warning Signs

Check any of the following that apply to you, and then check
your score at the end.

☐ During the past year I have missed an occasional dinner
with my family because I had to work late.

☐ During the past year I have not been physically present for
at least one birthday, holiday, or anniversary celebration
with my wife and children.

☐ During the past year our family did not have a vacation of
at least one week or longer.

☐ During the past year I have not spent a long weekend or
more alone with my wife.

☐ I do not know the names of my children's best friends.

☐ I do not have a weekly date with my wife.

☐ I do not experience at least a half hour of one-on-one time
with each of my children on a weekly basis.

☐ During the past year I have never canceled an important
meeting or business engagement so that I could spend
more time with my wife or family.

☐ When I travel I have missed at least one night of calling
back home to speak with my wife and children.

and was just starting to get better. As usual, we had been talking on the phone for hours, and I tried to convince her to allow me to bring her some food. At first, she wouldn't hear of it, but I persisted. I told her I wouldn't have to go inside but would just put the food on her doorstep and then leave. I must have worn her down, because she relented and gave me directions to her place. Then she gave me

☐ During the past year my wife has attended a parent-teacher event without me.

☐ It would be highly unusual for me to have lunch with my wife on a weekday unless we are on vacation or holiday.

☐ At least once during the past year my wife has expressed concern that I might be working too hard or traveling too much.

☐ During the past year my wife has not traveled with me on a business trip.

☐ During the past year I have missed at least one special school event for my children (soccer game, concert, awards banquet, etc.).

☐ When I travel alone I always leave an itinerary and contact information with my wife.

Scoring

If you checked ... then you are ...

0	either perfect or have a poor memory.
1–5	almost Superdad! Way to go!
6–10	pretty typical, so don't feel bad—there's hope!
11–15	in need of a vacation with this book.

her order: a salad from O'Charley's and one of those orange sherbet push-up popsicles. The salad was easy, but I hadn't seen one of those push-ups for years and pretty soon it was clear I was in trouble. I set out on a mad dash all over town, hitting five grocery stores before I found one. Racing to her apartment, I knew I must be in love, because for me, this was highly unusual behavior.

Even though you knew the honeymoon eventually would end, you did your best to carry the spirit of your wedding into your lives together. That first apartment was okay, but you took on extra projects at work to set aside money for a down payment on a house, not because anyone demanded it but because you wanted to give your sweetheart a nicer place to live.

Pretty soon, kids came along and you absolutely loved the idea of being a father. True, it was a little scary, but one thing was certain: you were going to do a better job being a father than your own dad. You remembered what it felt like when all the other kids got new bikes but you got a used one. You still felt the shame of wearing your older brother's hand-me-downs. So you pushed yourself harder at work to lead the sales team or produce the most widgets so that you had enough money to care for your family. True, sometimes all that work meant you got home late or didn't have time to help with homework, but you didn't complain. You had learned early on that money doesn't grow on trees, idle hands are the devil's tools, the early bird gets the worm, when the going gets tough the tough get going—all those good nuggets of wisdom we use to rationalize the long hours that sometimes get between us and those we love.

To compensate for your long hours and hard work—to say nothing of your growing absence—you rewarded yourself and your family with bigger and more expensive toys and experiences. Your reasoning made perfect sense: "If I can't actually be with my family as much as I want to, I can at least give them things that they will have fun with when we *are* together." But that backfired, because then you not only felt pressured to carve out more time with your family, but you also needed to get your money's worth from the boat, leading to conversations that went something like this:

She: "The kids just want to stay home this one weekend that you don't have to work."

He: "But I *bought* the boat so we could make the few weekends we have together more fun."

You thought the boat, the time-share in Orlando, and the skiing trip to Vail would give your kids great memories and make up for the times you had to be gone, and any hesitation from them or your wife made you feel a little resentful. So when your wife gently tried to suggest that you get rid of the time-share so you could spend that week hanging out with your son and maybe getting to know him better, you got a little defensive.

Remember when you worked overtime so you could take your sweetheart to a nice restaurant instead of Steak and Shake? Like I said, that should have been a clue. Your sweetheart most likely would have preferred spending those overtime hours with you, just sitting under a tree in the park. Ditto for your kids—all those long days to buy the bigger house and the nicer car and what they really wanted was to wrestle with you on the living room floor when you came home for dinner.

The Gravitational Pull of Success

I haven't met a single man who deliberately set out to make his career more important than his wife and family. And yet that is exactly what has happened to so many decent, good-hearted, and generous men. Change the details slightly, but the scenario I just sketched describes the lives of some of the men I know. It's as if success is to men as the moon is to the tides. Its pull is relentless, and eventually even the most well-intentioned man finds himself swept up in it.

Just as I was about to begin working on this book, I attended the funeral of my wife's great aunt and had the opportunity to get caught up with many of my cousins and other relatives. I'll never forget what one of my cousins said when I asked him how he was doing.

"You know, Louis," he began, "in many ways, things couldn't be better. We just moved into a new home in Atlanta, and because my job requires me to travel to Houston, my company purchased a luxury apartment for me when I'm there. And I was just offered a chance to become a partner in the firm I work for, which would make me a very rich man."

I was about to congratulate him, but he continued.

"And I'm just sick about it!"

"Huh? What do you mean?" I asked.

"Well here I am, making more money than I ever thought I would, with a dream house and two cars and three boys who I almost never see, and if I take the partnership, it will mean even more travel, along with a lot more money. I don't know *what* I'm going to do."

I told him not to take the offer, but I realize that none of us are wired to walk away from success. It's counterintuitive, which is why we have the term "golden handcuffs." Employers know that the best way to hold on to valuable employees is to offer them more money, more perks, and more prestige. It's the rare individual who can turn down a big raise even when it means our personal lives will suffer, and in my opinion, money is not the driving force behind a man's decision to work so hard. Rather, we want to do the right thing. We want to be responsible. We want to maximize the gifts that God has given us. We want to be industrious and ambitious. These are all positive values that we are taught all our lives, so we jump at each opportunity to move up the ladder in our careers because we have been conditioned to believe it is the responsible thing to do.

I know of a man who was successful in his line of work, but once he reached a certain level at his company, he was content to stay there. He was a regional sales rep and truly enjoyed calling on his customers and serving their needs. Because he was talented and productive, he was offered a promotion to vice president, but he initially turned it down because he would have to move his family to the company headquarters and he would have less contact with customers. At his next performance review, his supervisor warned him that by turning down a promotion he was viewed by senior management as lacking ambition. In so many words, the supervisor told him that it would be a bad career move to refuse the promotion. Suddenly he was worried that he might lose his job if he didn't take the promotion, and with his two sons about to enter college, he couldn't afford to beat the pavement looking for work. He became a vice president and made a lot more money, but the stress eventually spilled over into his home, causing severe problems in his marriage.

In addition to seeing career growth as the proper reward for our good work ethic, we live in a culture that places a high value on success. Our society judges you by what you accomplish and even to a certain extent by what you own. No one comes right out and says it, but living in the right neighborhood, driving the right kind of car, wearing the right kinds of clothes, and owning the latest gadgets and toys says a lot about who you are. If you don't *appear* successful then you must not *be* successful, and in our culture, success is everything. Unfortunately, many men buy into this thinking and focus all their time and energy on earning enough money to let everyone know they are successful, usually at the expense of those they love the most.

Now here's the rub. Intuitively, you probably already know that all the right things you are doing to provide for your family and enhance your standard of living actually are pulling you farther and farther away from them. Deep down inside you know what you need to do. But guess what? Your wife likes her nice house and your kids aren't about to give up their video games so that you all can be one big, happy, yet poor, family. All of your well-intentioned efforts to be a responsible husband and father have conditioned them to cope quite well with your absence.

There's Hope

So there you are, putting in sixty-hour weeks and feeling lousy because you had to be out of town on business on your daughter's birthday. You sense that your wife no longer thinks of you as her knight in shining armor, and the fact that she no longer complains when you get home late only confirms your fear that whatever spark is left in your marriage is about to go out. And what really frustrates you is that you're doing all this for *them*!

One of the crazy paradoxes of life is the way most married people look back on their days of having nothing as the happiest days of their lives. The converse can be just as paradoxical: the better off we are financially, the more miserable we are. A tiny apartment and eating canned soup was fine because you had each other. The reason you're having such a hard time in all the right things you're doing is that you have forgotten how much you need each other to be truly happy. You got married because you fell in love and you didn't want to go through life lonely. Now you're lonely because you're working so hard to provide for the people you love. You know exactly what you need to do to reclaim a dynamic relationship with your family, but you're afraid that if you cut back at work, you'll mess up your career.

Guess what? If you screw up a career, you can go back and fix it. If you mess up your kids' life or your marriage, for the most part the damage is permanent. One of the small blessings of getting down-sized is that people who have lost their jobs have discovered brand-new careers that they absolutely love. The truth is you got where you are by being reasonably intelligent, resourceful, and industrious, so even if you flat out quit your job to save your marriage, you will end up immeasurably happier with maybe a new, better job as a bonus.

I understand what you are feeling because I meet with people like you every week. I know that at times you may even feel like just giving up, like my friend Gerald, who confessed to me that he just wants to walk away from his wife and start over with someone else. So I will tell you what I told him: there's hope! Everything you have done that has brought you to this place can be used to take you to a better place. You are successful at work because you have put into place some best practices that have turned your customers and colleagues into raving fans. You know how to treat the key people at your job so that they feel like they are the most important people on earth.

Derrick "survived" his business trip to Paris. Who wouldn't? But he still felt increasingly disconnected from his family when I met with him. "I can't just quit this job so that I can spend more time with my family," he lamented.

"You don't have to," I reminded him. "But you might consider doing some of the things for them that you do for your best clients."

Throughout this book, I will be reminding you how those best practices at work have made you successful, then show you how to apply them to the people who matter most in your life. But first a question that I want you to think seriously and honestly about and that we will explore in the next chapter: what matters to you most?

3

What Matters
Most to You?

A T THE END OF THE PREVIOUS CHAPTER I ASKED YOU TO THINK seriously and honestly about what matters most to you. Another way to look at this question is this: when it comes right down to it, who or what would you be willing to die for?

I know your answers. Both of them: the very first answer you thought of, and then the real one. If you're like some of the guys I run into, your first answer is your family. Your wife, your kids, maybe your brothers and sisters or parents. I can almost guarantee that you would say the thing that matters most to you is your family, and I believe you. And you could probably back that statement up with dozens of examples of when you sacrificed for your family, put their needs over your own, and went the extra mile to demonstrate your love for them.

But there's a second answer, one that may not be spoken but is just as true as your first answer: your job. Again, I can almost guarantee you would never admit it. No one wants to acknowledge that they pay more attention to their work than to their families, but over and over again, without realizing it, we put our work ahead of everything until we wake up one day and discover the thing we thought mattered most to us now feels distant and unfamiliar. What's so insidious

39

is that no one deliberately sets out to honor his work over his family. And even as it is happening, we convince ourselves that it isn't:

"I feel awful about missing her soccer game, but if I didn't have this job, we couldn't afford to sign her up for the travel team."

"Sheila was so understanding about my missing dinner so many nights. I'm gonna surprise her Monday by bringing home some flowers."

"If I can just land this one major account, I'll be able to slow down a little and spend more time with my family."

That's probably what my friend Jim thought when he logged so many sixteen-hour days trying to close a major deal. The ultimate dealmaker, Jim now manages a multi-billion-dollar hedge fund because he never really slowed down after that major deal. Energized by his success and the affirmation from his managing partner, he dove in again and closed an even bigger deal. Along with each success came huge pay increases and bonuses, allowing him to move his family into a fabulous home with all of the features to keep his kids happy in his absence, including a swimming pool and a rec room complete with a huge widescreen television and a pool table.

I've known Jim for a long time and marveled at the way he seemed to balance his stressful career with his beautiful family. Isn't that the way it always is? We see another successful guy and wish we could be like him, feeling a little guilty about not being able to provide for our families as well as he does. So you can imagine my shock when Jim and I were having lunch and he sadly shared, "Louis, it just dawned on me that my daughter is leaving for college in twelve months and I don't really even know her!"

When I heard those words, it just broke my heart. Here's a guy who has it all and has worked hard and honestly to get it. He belongs to the right country club, drives a Porsche, has a beautiful wife and the greatest children you'll ever meet. If you asked him what he cares about most, I know he would say, "My wife and children," and that all his hard work is for them. And yet what has he really given those that matter most to him? Absence. His oldest daughter was starting her senior year in high school, and by his own admission he didn't really know her. He didn't know what kind of music she enjoyed listening to. Her favorite movie. What she liked doing with her friends. What she wanted to study in college. What she thought about God and church. He loved her, no question. But he never really got fully involved in her life because he was always chasing the next deal so that he could give her and the rest of his family a better life.

I have to give Jim credit, though, and this should encourage all of you as well. Once he realized he had let seventeen years slip by so quickly, he put the brakes on his career so that for at least her last year at home he would be more present in her life. It's never too late to show your wife and children that they are your most important customers.

"I've got twelve months before she's gone for good," he told me. "All I've ever known how to do is build businesses, and every business I built started with a business plan. So I'm going to put together a twelve-month plan to regain her heart before she leaves. Her needs will come before my business. In fact, her needs will *be* my business. No more sixteen-hour days and sneaking in to kiss her after she's already fallen asleep. No more being clueless about her hopes and dreams. I'm not sure I can make up for seventeen years in twelve months, but I'm going to try."

By the way, you might be tempted to think that putting work ahead of family happens only with hard-charging entrepreneurs like my friend Jim, that this is a problem only for people with lots of money. Trust me, confusion over what matters most to a guy is not a money issue. It's a balance issue. It's the normal and honorable desire to provide for your loved ones, but spun out of control. Remember, my father was not a wealthy man but a construction worker who wanted to do a better job of providing for his family. When he started his own company, we were all so proud of him, even if it meant long hours away from us. Many times, his work took him out of town and he would be home only on weekends, but we knew he was doing it for us. I don't know how my mom managed it, but somehow she

Reengineering Your Work Life

As you refocus on what matters most to you, something will have to give. Trying to pay more attention to your wife and family without changing anything at work is a recipe for burnout. Here are some options to consider.

Put family events on your work calendar. We often miss out on family activities because we forget about them. Then once our work obligations get on our calendars, it's too late to make changes. If you have an 11:45 lunch date with your wife on your calendar, it gives you a good excuse when someone at work tries to schedule a meeting during that time: "We need to find another day because I have a commitment."

Negotiate with your employer or colleagues. Many of us are too timid about asking for time off to attend important family events. You may be surprised to learn that your employer will be generous about these issues. Talk to your supervisor or colleagues. Offer to make up the time missed or cover for one of them when they need time off. Let your company know that your family is important to you; if you are a valued employee, they will find ways to support that.

Know what's expected of you. If you hold a salaried position, what is your company's expectation regarding the average number of hours you work each week? If it's fifty and made it to every one of the athletic events and other activities that the six of us kids were involved in. I later learned that she would show up for a game and stay just long enough for us to see her and know she was there. Then it was off to another kid's activity so that

you have to work sixty or seventy hours for a few weeks to meet a deadline, many companies will allow "comp time." Take it.

Work smarter. Most studies of employees who complain of overwork find that they often work harder because they are inefficient. Do you delegate whenever you can? Would some training in technology help you utilize tools designed to reduce your workload? Do you procrastinate and then have to work long hours to catch up? A supervisor, colleague, or HR person might be able to help you find ways to work smarter and free up more time.

Downsize your job. If you are consistently working long hours and missing weekends because of work, make a creative offer to your employer: "I will take a 10 percent pay cut if you will let me cut back to forty hours and give some of my responsibilities to someone else."

Change jobs. Changing jobs is always a risk, especially if the job market is sluggish. But if the people who matter most to you are at risk, a new, less stressful job might be in order. Be open with your employer: "I love working here, but it's taking a toll on my family." If you are a valuable employee, they may counter with a redesigned work assignment.

even though all six of us may have been performing or competing on the same day, we all knew she was there. And while I loved seeing her, it would have been nice to see my dad now and then, but he just couldn't afford to come.

I am convinced that when Jim was starting out in his business, he believed all his hard work was for those he cared about so much: his wife and children. Yet there comes a point for all of us when the pleasure we get from our success takes over, replacing our spouses and children in our hierarchy of priorities. I have seen this happen with both men and women from all walks of life, regardless of their net worth.

Knowing Jim as I do, he will definitely make an impact on his daughter's life in those twelve months. He didn't come right out and say it, but his daughter just became his most important customer. He will unleash all the skill, knowledge, talent, and perseverance he has used to build a successful business. You don't need new, unfamiliar knowledge to reclaim your relationships with those who matter to you most. You don't need to sign up for a special program or seminar to learn how to restore your spouse or children to their rightful place in your life. All you need to do is treat them with the same respect and honor as you treat your customers, and in the remaining chapters we'll look more specifically at how to do that.

But first, you need to establish what matters most to you and why.

How Success Seduces

Before I met my wife, I had what could easily be called the dream job for any young man. I worked in the music industry as a behind-the-scenes guy making sure concert venues were booked, equipment arrived on time, the media got their interviews, and the musicians were cared for. I was young, single, and working closely with some of my heroes: Gladys Knight, Luther Vandross, Wynonna Judd, Whitney Houston, BeBe Winans, and producer David Foster. Imagine sitting in Dionne Warwick's kitchen and having lunch in her home. Or being invited to Oprah's home. Or sitting next to Halle Berry at the Grammy Awards. I mean, these are people I'd watched on television, and now they invited me into their homes. Sometimes I had to pinch myself to make sure I wasn't dreaming.

When I first got that job, though, it was just a way to earn a living. Yes, it was an attractive job, but as far as I was concerned it was an exciting way to earn a living. I wasn't thinking about career or success; I was thinking about making enough money to pay the bills and maybe have a little left over. If you had asked me then what mattered to me most, I would have said things like my family, my friends, and having a good time. I probably wouldn't have said, "This job is going to be the most important thing in life to me." No one really starts a career thinking that way. It's a job. We want to do our best at it, but we usually keep it in perspective at first.

Yet it wasn't long before that career took on a life of its own. It turned out that I was making more than a living; the money was more than I had ever made up to that point in my life. Being able to travel all over the world on someone else's dime was an attractive benefit. I enjoyed a nice middle-class childhood, but I have to tell you, staying in five-star hotels often seemed surreal. I would look at the room rate when I checked in and see that it was almost the same as my monthly condo payment of six hundred dollars! And many times when I traveled I didn't have to worry about reserving a rental car because a limo picked us up at the airport. All of this, plus I got to hang out with such great and interesting people. What began as a job turned into something bigger and more consuming than I ever could have imagined.

Then something happened. I had an "ah-ha" moment after working in this area of business for several years. All I can remember is that it was January, and suddenly it was January again. A brand new year. I should have been happy, but I was beginning to evaluate. An entire year had just passed in what seemed like the snap of a finger, and I barely knew whether I was coming or going. Despite being a pretty well-rounded guy, it dawned on me that for the past twelve months, I really didn't have a life. I was on call 24/7 and often was still in the studio at three in the morning. The names changed, but not the routine: Hop on a plane to LA. Catch a ride to the studio to do a recording with Whitney Houston or some other major recording artist. Fly back to an empty condo and get ready to do it all over again. Work had become so important that I began to have an internal battle over what really mattered to me.

Bob Buford, in his classic book, *Halftime*, writes of listening to that "still small voice," and it must have been that voice that spoke to me: This isn't right. You can't live like this. Something's got to give, and the result may not be pretty.

I made a change.

Mind you, I needed an income. I wasn't independently wealthy and didn't have a big nest egg to support me while I tried to figure out what to do with my life. Plus, I was giving up something most people would die for: access. Talk about a struggle. A very loud voice was telling me, "Louis, you're nuts!" while that quieter voice was saying, "I have something better for you."

Deep down inside, most people know what really matters most to them, but the allure of success is just too strong. I recall hearing about a well-known former diplomat and media magnate who sensed the still small voice telling him to leave a lucrative but stressful career, and yet his biggest worry was that if he did leave, no one would ever return his calls again. Even if that were true (and it usually isn't), which is worse? Losing access to your colleagues in the work world, or losing access to your wife and children? How would you feel if those who really matter most to you never returned your calls?

The truth is, if someone's worth to you is dependent on the title on his or her business card, how valuable to you are they, really? If they lose interest in you because you have downsized to a less important and less consuming position, are they really worth all that you do for them? Unfortunately, we tend to value people for what they do rather than for who they are. Ever notice how people will ask you, "What do you do?" I don't recall anyone asking me who I am, but isn't that what really defines us as individuals? But because we place so much emphasis on jobs and titles, we let customers and clients and colleagues become more important than the people we live with.

I have to admit that I loved my experiences in the music business, not just because of all the obvious perks but also because I came to respect the majority of the musicians I worked with and couldn't imagine not being a part of their lives. They were just as classy off-stage as they were on, and part of me worried that I was making a big mistake walking away from them. But another part of me knew that other things mattered more to me than hanging out with famous people. Like having a wife and starting a family. I knew that the lifestyle required by that job would never work in a marriage. I wanted to have children, and I wanted to have someone to pour into and then have someone to pour back into me. As much as I enjoyed the travel and the people and the whole atmosphere of my job, I knew I wouldn't find what truly mattered to me there.

I'm a huge believer in Providence, and I believe that for some reason God wanted to teach me what matters most to me *before* I got married. Maybe he knew how easily I could get distracted by success and gave me that one fast-paced and seemingly enviable job to show me that work—even meaningful, enjoyable work—will never fully satisfy my heart's desire. I shudder to think what might have happened if I took that job shortly after marrying Charita. Nothing would have convinced me that anything could be more important than her, but a dream job like that surely would have ruined our marriage. I know because I saw so many decent people around me who could not prevent themselves from making their work the most important thing in their lives. That's not to say I haven't had to stop and rearrange my priorities from time to time. I have. Our work—especially work that we enjoy and is fulfilling—can be insidious in the way it nudges our loved ones out of the way. In most cases, we don't actually choose our work over our familes but rather allow it to consume us, almost by default. If I don't stop and reset the default switch, I'm as capable as the next guy of letting things get out of balance.

Working Hard and Enjoying It Less

Even if you aren't wired to be seduced by success, it's hard to escape the influence of the company you work for. Not to blame corporate America, but it's a rare company that encourages men to put their families first. Here too it's a subtle rather than a direct attack. No one in management is going to come right out and say, "I really don't care if your son is having his first football game this afternoon, you have a job to do and it's right here!" But when you try to rearrange your schedule to make that game, you seldom get a pat on the back. More often than not, your boss will find a way to let you know your absence from the budget meeting did not go unnoticed by *his* boss. It takes only one half-serious or even joking reprisal for leaving early for a family matter to train a good employee: it better not happen very often.

Let me give you another example of how companies inadvertently force men to make their jobs the thing that matters most to them. A friend of mine, I'll call him Donnie, works as a sales rep in the pharmaceutical business. He's on the road a lot, often traveling with a small team that makes presentations at hospitals and medical centers all over the country. It's a lucrative yet competitive business with a lot at stake. That environment alone is enough to put strain on a guy's family, but there are added pressures.

"After a long day making presentations and answering questions from our clients, we're all expected to meet the boss in the hotel bar for drinks," he explained. "Then it's off as a group to a fabulous restaurant for an expensive meal with more drinks. Of course, no one forces you to drink, but who wants to be the party pooper? Sometimes, we then head to a club where everyone is dancing. Between the alcohol, the cozy atmosphere, and maybe a dance with one of your colleagues, it can take its toll. Especially when the company sends you on the road for days at a time and then expects you to put in long hours doing paperwork between trips."

I don't mean to pick on the pharmaceutical industry; this happens in just about any business that requires employees to travel. And its a rare individual who can spurn the boss's invitation and spend the night alone in his hotel room. I'm not blaming companies; they probably think they're rewarding their top employees by helping them let their hair down a bit. They realize that business travel is stressful, and therefore they offer generous expense accounts as a way of recruiting and holding on to talented employees. And I'm also not excusing guys who get caught up in behavior that puts their marriages at risk. They should know better. This is simply the reality of working in the corporate environment, but it takes its toll on families. You better remember how important your wife is when you are sitting across the table from an attractive colleague in a five-star restaurant in Manhattan.

Work *Is* Important

There's yet another reason why we are inclined to make work more important than our families. Most of us learn from our fathers and others that part of being a responsible adult is to go to work every day. Whether you carry a lunch box or a briefcase, there's something noble and right about work. Some may argue with me about this, but

I believe men feel a greater degree of pressure to earn a decent living so that they can provide for their families. Certainly, women feel this too, but for a man—rightly or wrongly—this sense of responsibility is stronger, which sets us up for letting our work become more important than it should be.

I have a close friend who has agonized recently over the way he has poured himself into his career. His kids are grown and doing well, yet he worries that he might have let his work take priority over his family. A wonderful and compassionate gentleman, this guy has worked in Christian ministry all his life, enriching the lives of others, often traveling all over the world to help advance the gospel. We were discussing this recently and he told me that the one piece of advice he remembers most from his father just before he got married is this: "Remember, work is the most important thing you can do." And he offered that advice not just once but almost every time they talked. His dad was not a coldhearted, materialistic person, but he lived through the Depression and wanted to make sure his son was prepared in case another financial crisis struck our nation. And my friend, being a good son, wanted to honor his father, so when he began his career, he made sure he always gave his best, contributing above and beyond what was expected of him, and this is a perfect storm for transforming work from a necessary and noble activity to an all-encompassing drive that gradually separates us from our families.

My friend's story rings true for me. I have seen many pastors lose their families because they were so devoted to the church. These are men who put in eighteen- to twenty-hour days building their churches, which is really crazy when you think about it. It's little wonder that so many of the teenaged children of these pastors turned their backs on the church, because in their tender minds, it was the church that robbed them of time with their daddies.

This is exacerbated by what have become known as the helping professions: medicine, education, law enforcement, social services, and Christian ministry. In these cases, it's not society or other influences that lead a man to make his work his god; rather it's a self-imposed belief that his calling is indeed more noble because people's lives are at stake, therefore his family has to accept his absence without complaint. As my friend explained, "I missed birthdays and sporting events and vacations because I was doing 'the Lord's work' and thought that made it okay." In other words, a son learns that his choir concert is not nearly as important as the brain surgery his father had to perform that night.

It doesn't take much for us to believe that the work we do is so important that it justifies our having little time, energy, and attention left over to give our families.

Your Most Valuable Customers

The challenge, of course, is to find the balance between your work customers and your spouse and family. Easier said than done. As I've said, no one sets out to put his work ahead of his family. Quite the contrary, most of us start out with our priorities in order and a strong resolve never to let anything come between us and our families. So how do you return your spouse and children to that prominent position in your life as your priority customers? Here are a few suggestions to help you keep your priorities in order.

Fight amnesia. Isn't it amazing how quickly we forget the thrill of that first kiss? Nothing could stand in the way of that date with the woman you fell in love with. Boss offers you overtime? Forget it. A blizzard closes highways and makes driving treacherous? Get out the snowshoes, because I want to be with my baby tonight. Sometimes you just need to turn back the clock and reflect on why your wife or children were so important to you at one time. You worked so hard to gain their love. Why? And why let something as fleeting as a job become more important to you?

Use your imagination. Imagine what it would be like to come home to an empty house or apartment. How would you feel if another man began providing better "customer service" to your wife? Now imagine how things would be different for you if your wife felt she was the most important thing in the world to you. Imagine how your son might react if you cut short a business trip and surprised him by showing up for his tennis match. Imagine receiving an award from one of your top customers. How would you feel if that award came from your family?

Keep the brand alive. No doubt, many of your key customers make sure you know their brand. They give you coffee mugs and paperweights and luggage tags with their logos on them. They want to make sure you never forget they exist. So keep your family's "brand" with you wherever you go. I always travel with a photo of my family that I display prominently in my hotel room to remind me what matters most. Keep their photos on your desk at work. Tack your child's drawings to your bulletin board in your office. Ask your wife to seal a note in an envelope that you can read when you get on the plane. These may seem like small things, but they serve the same purpose as all that branding from your other customers. They say, "I matter to you!"

Play hookey. If you are a manager or supervisor and have the freedom to do so, every now and then let your staff know you're skipping out for the afternoon to spend time with your wife or children. This sends a message to your colleagues and your family that family is more important than work, and most workers will show greater respect toward a leader who is a family man. It also sends a message to yourself: "I can do this and still do my job well." I realize that depending on your line of work, you may not be able to do this easily. If you're a brain surgeon, you can't really hand your scalpel over to a nurse and tell her to finish up because you want to make your daughter's swim meet. And if you're an hourly worker, punching out early may not be allowed. However, with some planning, most people are able to change their work schedules by using personal days or even agreeing to forego a couple of hours of pay to leave early. In these cases, your sacrifice sends an even more powerful message to others that family is important to you.

Go low tech. Cell phones, texting, and email are great ways to stay in touch with your wife and children when you travel. But the next time you check in to your hotel, take out the folder of hotel stationery and write letters to each of your family members. Sure, you'll probably get home before the letters arrive, but "real mail" will tell your most valued customers in a special way that they matter. And the act of sitting down and writing those letters will keep your family at the top of your priorities, because you don't do this for just anybody.

Give yourself permission. My friend in Christian ministry shared with me that his wake-up call came from another pastor who knew of his struggle and told him, "I give you permission to put your wife and family ahead of the church." Sounds simple, but sometimes we just need to give ourselves permission to do what we know is right. Your job is not your boss. Your *boss* is not your boss. *You* are, so give yourself permission to let your family matter more to you than anything.

Be Reasonable with Yourself

A generation ago, more women were beginning to enter the workplace, and their concerns over some of these same issues created something of a monster: Supermom! Women began having nervous breakdowns because they were trying to break the glass ceiling at work while attending every school event for their children, plus giving their husbands the attention they deserved. You could always recognize a Supermom by the grim look on her face as she was doing something fun with her daughter at the park! (In fairness to women, isn't it interesting that they automatically assumed that they, not their husbands, had to balance work and family? For whatever reason, these women generally poured themselves into both their careers and their homes.)

So a word of caution. You can't be Superdad. He doesn't exist, just as Supermom is a fantasy. You cannot avoid missing an event in your wife or child's life. For one thing, you probably plan six to nine months out at work, so if a teacher sends home a note inviting you to storytime at your third-grader's classroom in two weeks, it's unrealistic to expect you to cancel something that has been on your calendar for so long. You also need to be reasonable about what kinds of things require your presence. If your daughter has dance classes with one big dance recital for the year, you probably don't want to miss that. But if she also plays soccer and has two games a week for the three-month season, missing a soccer game or two is understandable.

There's also a big difference between presence and attendance. I know some dads who show up at every little event in their children's lives, but they aren't really present because they're working their Blackberries the whole time. If your son looks toward the sidelines and sees you checking your email, you might as well be back at the office. Even if you have to miss a few events, your kids will always appreciate your being actively engaged at the events you do attend.

Finally, your well-intentioned efforts to shower your wife with more attention could be more of a shock to her system than she's ready to handle. Chances are she has learned to cope with your absence by filling her life with other activities, activities that she may really enjoy. Before you start planning a lot of time together, talk to her. Let her know you've been reevaluating your priorities and that you hope to regain some balance in your life. Thank her for the many times she has had to go alone to school events or spend a weekend with you out of town. Apologize for putting your work ahead of her and invite her input on how to reconnect. You started your lives together as a team, so enter this new adventure as a team as well.

I *know* that your wife and children mean more to you than anything. You know it too. But as we race through life doing our best to provide for them, it's easy to lose our focus, to let our work, our titles, our success, and our colleagues creep into that sacred space that has been reserved for what matters most. As that happens, we put distance between ourselves and our families and actually become closer to our customers at work. That's what happened to my friend Jim, who suddenly realized he didn't really know his seventeen-year-old daughter.

Do you really know your most valuable customers? We'll find out in the next chapter.

4

Do You Really
Know Your Customer?

ANYONE IN SALES WILL TELL YOU THAT THE BEST WAY TO GAIN A competitive edge is to know your customer. If you manufacture a product, your customer is usually a retailer—a store that sells your product to consumers. And if you're a retailer, your customer is the consumer—the person who buys a product you carry. Regardless of the size of the business or the nature of the product, your success depends on how well you know your customer.

In the music business, major labels try to learn as much as they can about their major retailers, such as Best Buy or Barnes and Noble, so that they can serve them better. Initially, those big retailers were reluctant to provide a lot of information to these companies, and you can understand why. The music publishers basically were asking to look at the financial books to see what was selling and what wasn't, and for years retailers viewed this as proprietary information. But eventually the retailers relented and began giving more information to sales executives at the music publishing companies. In fact, they even went a step farther and selected various music companies to serve as "category captains." A category captain was given the opportunity to determine the product mix in a given category of music—rock, blues, jazz, country, and so on. And those category captains were given unprecedented access to the retailers' sales data, and then analyzed it and basically told the retailers which CDs to stock in that category.

I asked a friend who is familiar with this category-captain concept why a retailer would let one vendor gather so much valuable and often secret information about their store, and his answer made a lot of sense. "The more information you have about your customer, the better chance you have to help him be successful." He said that in sales, you can't just think about yourself and how much you want to make a big sale. "If I can help my customer become successful, the sales will follow."

From my own experience as an entrepreneur, I have learned the truth of this statement. A lot of what I do is to help businesses find ways to partner on projects that become winners for all parties involved. My ultimate goal is for them to enjoy the highest degree of success possible. So whenever I begin a new venture, I try to learn as much as I can about the companies and individuals I will be working with — my customers. We call it the fact-finding phase of the project, and it involves trying to discover what their business goals are — what they hope to achieve in the venture. But I also try to drill down on other things, like what's important to them, what motivates them, what they are passionate about, and what their dreams are. And even if it's a company I've done business with before, I try to keep learning about them because I know that businesses change over time.

All of this fact-finding and trying to understand our customers takes a lot of time, and as you know, in any business, time is money. If occasionally I am tempted to forego this time-consuming and expensive process, I think of some of my competitors who jumped into relationships without really knowing their customers very well. The resulting disasters are enough to keep me studying my customers. I can't afford to fail, and I believe one of the reasons my business has succeeded is that I know my customers well.

The lesson here for me as a husband and father is clear: I have to know my family well too if I want to see success in the form of a happy home.

Mr. and Mrs. Customer

When I first started talking about this book to some friends, I discovered an interesting reaction. Guys heard the title and said, "That's me!" Women heard the title and immediately got it: "I've gotta get that for my husband." Just recently, I was talking to a woman — the CEO of a small company — who had heard I was writing a book and asked about it. When I explained the concept, she became quite animated. "I remember being so angry with my husband once that I actually wrote him a memo requesting a 'business meeting' and even included an agenda. It was the only way I could get his attention!"

Whenever I've talked about this book to women, the response is always a variation of this: "I'd love it if my husband would treat me at *least* as well as he treats the people in his work world!" Occasionally, a woman would say, "We *both* need this book." In those cases, both the husband and wife had challenging jobs that tended to pull them from each other and their families. So let's talk a little about this whole concept of your spouse and children being your customers.

I know that most men want to be just as successful at home as they are at work. And initially, you wouldn't *think* of calling your wife or children customers. They are so much more than that, right? I mean, you need your work world so you can earn a decent living, but you don't *love* your customers and colleagues. You don't live with them, vacation with them, or sleep with them. Your wife and children are flesh and blood, while your customers are, well, customers. In your hierarchy of importance, your wife and children are at the very top, right?

Sort of.

While it's true that you love your wife and children but only work with your customers, your behavior often sends signals to your loved ones that your customers matter more than they do. That is why the cry of a woman's heart is often, "Please, you don't have to be perfect, but give me the same respect you give your people at work." And that's really sad when you stop to think about it, because in a way, she is settling for something less than what she deserves; those you love should expect to be treated *better* than the way you treat your customers and work colleagues. So really, I'm setting the bar kind of low for you, but I can almost guarantee that if you begin thinking of your loved ones as your customers, they will become your *best* customers and you will begin to feel like the hero you want to be to them.

Building a Customer Profile

I have a friend who signed up to be an Amway salesperson while he was still in college. He met with his direct distributor, who gave him his sales kit with samples of products, order forms, and a small supply of index cards to record information about each customer. He set out on foot in his neighborhood, going door to door trying to sell SA-8 laundry detergent and other cleaning products, and after that first day he dutifully sat down and filled out his order forms and wrote down information about his new customers on the little index cards. But, as he related to me, that lasted for about a week. "What seemed glamorous at first became a chore, so I quit altogether." Not surprisingly, he's no longer in sales.

But he made the mistake a lot of men make when it comes to getting to know their best customers — their wives and children. I'll bet that within a few weeks of that first date with the woman who is now your wife, you knew her favorite color, her favorite meal, and her favorite song. You paid attention to things like what made her laugh and what made her sad, and you did the things that made her laugh and tried not to do the things that made her sad. You knew whether she liked flowers or chocolates, jewelry or stuffed animals. As your courtship progressed and you realized you might be spending the rest of your life with her, you got to know what she thought of certain social issues, whether she tended to vote Democrat or Republican, what church she attended, and her thoughts about faith.

In other words, you began building a customer profile for this person who at that moment was the most important person in the world to you. And while you probably didn't record that data on little index cards or on a spreadsheet, you filed it away in your brain and retrieved it faster than a high-speed computer when you needed it:

"Louis, let's go to a movie this weekend."

"Sure—there's a new one with Sandra Bullock. I think she's your favorite actress."

"Wow! You remembered. Oh Louis, you're so sweet."

Building a customer profile has its rewards.

One of the challenges in customer relations comes with our oldest, most loyal customers. The tendency is to put your relationships with those customers on autopilot and just watch the business continue to grow. The problem is that customers change. Their business plans adapt to consumer needs and market conditions. New people move into positions of leadership. If you don't continue to build and update their profiles, your customers eventually become strangers. You don't know the new people, the new direction, or the new needs.

That happens in marriage all too often. When you're dating that girl who you're pretty sure is going to be your wife, you are so close to that you can finish each other's sentences. By the time you are married, you really do know her well—probably better than anyone else. And in those early years of marriage, especially if you haven't started a family yet, you continue to grow in your knowledge of each other. But then, your other customers begin to demand more attention. As an energetic and enterprising employee, you move up the ladder, and each position brings more responsibility along with the bigger paycheck. Initially, you get a lot of affirmation from your wife for these promotions, which fuels your natural desire to excel. But at some point—and it's different for everyone—you're paying more attention to your work customers than your primary customer at home. It's not intentional, but it's insidious, creeping into your life without your even noticing it, as it did with Nick.

Nick married Sherri, his high school sweetheart, right after he graduated from college. As an engineer, he started out in an entry level position in a large company, the sort of company in which you spend your first two or three years doing the dirty work no one else wants to do. It was uninspiring work for the young engineer, but the one advantage was that the hours were pretty regular, so Nick

How Well Do You Know Your Wife?

With apologies to the old *Newlywed Game*, here's a short quiz to help you determine if your "customer database" is up-to-date. Answer the following questions, then show your answers to your wife. Then ask her to answer the same questions about you and compare answers. Were you surprised at how you did? How do people learn these types of things about each other?

1. What is your spouse's favorite television program?

2. If you asked your spouse where he or she would like to spend a two-week vacation, where would it be?

3. If your spouse has thirty minutes of free time during a day, what would he or she most likely do during that time?

4. What household chore does your spouse dislike the most?

and Sherri were always together every evening and on weekends. In addition to protecting one night each week as their date night, they were practically inseparable. One of their favorite things to do together was to take a nightly walk around a little lake in a park near their house. It was on those walks that Nick unknowingly updated his customer profile as he and his wife shared everything from what happened that day to their dreams for the future.

When Nick got his first promotion, he called Sherri right from his office because he was so excited and wanted to share the good news with his best friend. By the time he got home that night, she had already made reservations at their favorite restaurant and even had a little gift wrapped for him. As they ate, they talked about what they would do with all that extra money from the raise that went

5. If your spouse works outside the home, name one of his or her colleagues from work. If your spouse doesn't work outside the home, name the person he or she would most likely meet for coffee.

6. Name the last book your spouse read.

7. What is your spouse's favorite "guilty pleasure" food (chocolate, sushi, cheesecake, etc.)?

8. If you and your family could live anywhere in the world, where would your spouse choose to live?

9. What's the one thing you do that annoys your spouse the most?

10. During the past week, what was your spouse's happiest moment?

with the promotion, and you couldn't have found any happier people on the planet.

Fast-forward about five years, and Nick is feeling frustrated. He can't really explain it other than to say he feels as if he barely knows his wife. "She's not the same person," he complains. "It's almost like she's jealous whenever I get another promotion. And even though I go out of my way on a business trip to bring home something that I know she loves, she says she wishes I didn't have to travel as much."

I don't know Nick personally; I heard his story from a friend. But I think he's absolutely right. His wife is not the same person. Like all of us, she has changed, but Nick is still using his old customer profile. Once he began getting promotions and building his career, he quit paying attention to the little things. He had to, because his work was also more demanding. Longer hours. Travel. Whereas he once was home every night at five and could sit around the dinner table getting caught up, he now has to stay at the office longer, and when he does get home, he's in another zone and not really in any frame of mind to listen to how his wife's day went. And trust me, stopping at an airport gift shop to bring something home just doesn't cut it. He thinks he's being thoughtful, but his wife sees it almost as an insult.

He's doing great at work because he has learned exactly what his customers need and does everything to help them meet those needs. He's doing poorly at home because he doesn't know his most important customer as well as he once did.

Holding on to Your Most Loyal Customer

If I ever get too far removed from one of my customers or business colleagues, the worst thing I can do is just ignore the problem and hope they don't leave for one of my competitors. However, when you get to that place in business, the temptation is to do just that. You're embarrassed and don't really want to face your customer, or it just seems like too much work, so you're tempted to procrastinate or just move on. Instead, I have to swallow my pride a little, get an appointment with that customer, and just put the cards on the table: "Hey, we haven't been paying enough attention to you lately, and I'm sure it shows in the way we are serving you. I'm here to tell you we're going to start treating you like a brand new account and get things back on track again."

And that's exactly what we need to do when we have lost touch with our families. There's no perfect way to do this, but the following steps will help you begin to reconnect with your most important customer.

Lean into the problem. The best leaders I know never hesitate to admit they are wrong or that they've made a mistake, and they don't waste any time doing it. Instead of avoiding problems, they lean into them. Surprise your wife and ask her to pick a day when she can meet you for lunch. Then put your cards on the table, so to speak. Thank her for meeting you and tell her you know that you've let too many things interfere with your relationship with her and your children. Tell her you want to make some changes but that you want her input. Then invite her to say whatever she wants.

Don't just listen. It's one thing to listen to your customers. But if you don't follow through on what they say, they will take their business elsewhere. If a colleague asks for my input, I'm always impressed when he pulls out a piece of paper and takes notes. It shows me that he values what I have to say. It may seem awkward, but when you ask for your wife's input on the changes she'd like to see, write them down. If she seems taken aback by that, explain that you're serious about this and that she's as important as any client, with whom you would do the same thing.

Rebuild your customer profile. The sidebar on pages 62–63 will give you a pretty good idea of how well you know your wife. It's actually a fun, nonthreatening way to show your wife that you want to know her better. Knowing her favorite movie won't undo years of neglect, but it opens the door for other questions and conversations that can help you reconnect. When you go to the movies, take time afterward for coffee or dessert and ask her what she thinks about it, which character she likes the best and why, how she would have handled things if she were the female lead. Why? First, because that's how you got to know her in the first place. But more important, this is how you rebuild your profile. These conversations go beneath the surface and give you a clearer picture of who your wife really is.

Be prepared. When a sales rep has to meet with three different customers in a day, he tries to spend a little time before each appointment going over his file on the customer just to make sure he's prepared. It helps him address the customer's unique needs and give that customer his full attention. Sometimes the transition from the office to home is clouded with the things that are on your mind from work, causing you to let them creep into your relationships with your family. You wouldn't think of walking into a business appointment and talking about the meeting you just had with another customer, but that's often what we do when we walk in the door after a long day at the office. Use your drive home to prepare for what you really want when you get home: an enjoyable experience with the people you love. Reflect on your wife, her needs, hopes, and dreams. Focus on your kids and think of what their day at school was like. Mentally page through your profile about your wife and children to prepare for a great "appointment" with them.

More Than a Customer

I know this business language might seem inappropriate when thinking about your loved ones, and in a way it is. Time spent with your family is not really an appointment, and all that you know about them is much more than a profile. But it's the language we use fifty to sixty hours a week, and sometimes our language dictates to us what is most important. If your family doesn't have a slot in your calendar or a file in your customer database, they might not get the attention they deserve. It's strange how that works, which is why we are going to undo all of that by learning how to treat the people we love as if they were our customers.

5

Customer Communication Strategies

I N THE CLASSIC DRAMA *COOL HAND LUKE*—A MOVIE MADE WELL before my time, by the way—Luke, a reprobate prisoner played by the late Paul Newman, has just gotten caught after escaping from the prison chain gang. A charmingly disrespectful inmate with a knack for getting himself in hot water with prison authorities, he unwisely yet characteristically mocks the despotic prison captain, who is sarcastically welcoming the escapee back to the chain gang. Obviously unimpressed with Luke's impudence, the captain sends him gasping to the ground with a savage blow, then regains his composure and utters these now famous words: "What we have here is a failure to communicate."

Poor communication may not always result in getting your lights punched out, but it's certain to wreak havoc in the business world. According to Robert Kent, former dean of Harvard Business School, "In business, communication is everything."[1] Approximately 70 to 80 percent of what most managers do in the business world is some form of communication, written or oral. Think of how much time you spend on the phone, checking email, responding to text messages, or creating reports and presentations for meetings. Every day, we communicate with our colleagues, with those who report to us, with those to whom we report, with vendors, and with customers.

If you do not learn how to communicate effectively in your career, you won't last very long, because you won't be successful. Consider this scenario in the music business. The business manager emails the director of sales forecasting and asks for her first three months' forecast on a particular album. She emails back: 50,000. He then emails the production manager, who's waiting to place an order on that CD with the company who will manufacture it. For whatever reason, the production manager sees 500,000 instead of 50,000 and places the order. Two weeks later the inventory control manager calls the business manager wondering why a shipment of 500,000 CDs arrived when he was expecting 50,000.

How Not to Communicate

Can you imagine ever shouting at your best customer? Of course not. Here are some other communication killers you would never do at work and shouldn't do at home either.

1. *Beginning sentences with "You never" or "You always."* It always puts the other person on the defensive, and it's almost never true.

2. *Blaming others when you are criticized.* Taking responsibility is a sign of maturity and confidence and makes it hard for arguments to get started.

3. *Rehashing past offenses.* Do you constantly remind a customer of the time he screwed up an order? Of course not, nor should you do it at home. At the very best, it will shut down communication, but most likely it will start an argument.

What we have here is a failure to communicate effectively, and it is costing this company hundreds of thousands of dollars. It might even cost someone his job. All because of a one-digit error. It's for this reason that businesses spend billions of dollars each year providing training to help their employees do a better job communicating. The National Commission on Writing estimates that American businesses spend 3.1 billion dollars annually just on improving the written communication skills of its employees. Your success in your career depends on the extent to which you effectively and consistently communicate with your colleagues and customers.

In my experience in the corporate world, communication often breaks down during two times: when things are going really well and when things are going poorly. If you have an account that is

4. *Using sarcasm.* In a meeting with your most profitable customer, she offers a suggestion and you reply, "That might work if our goal were to go bankrupt." Hardly! Guys sometimes think a sarcastic comment is funny, but usually only one person laughs.

5. *Pouting.* Men don't really pout. We just use the silent treatment when our feelings are hurt. Not a great way to promote good communication in a marriage. Would you do that if an important customer said something you didn't like? If your wife treads onto a sensitive subject, suck it up. Better to just admit your feelings are hurt than to pout.

profitable and everything seems to be on track with them, it's easy to ignore them so that you can focus elsewhere. However, that lack of communication can appear to that account to be arrogance or a sign that you just don't care. On the other hand, when an account is experiencing huge problems, isn't making much money for you, and starts calling you every day to see what's going on, some companies take the "out of sight, out of mind" approach, hoping the problem will go away on its own. (It never does.)

The truth is, however, that you need to communicate well when things are going really well, when they are tanking, and anytime in between. In business, there is no good time to ease up on communication. It is the lifeblood of a successful business.

The Business of Marriage

The reason we work so hard at communication in our careers is that we know what happens when we lose touch with our customers. Regular communication is one way we show those customers that they are important, that they matter to us. I know some companies that establish a "communications protocol"—a schedule for when to communicate to a customer as well as when to use the various types of communication needed to maintain a healthy relationship with that customer. If this is so important in business, it ought to be even more important in our marriage and family relationships. In fact, most counselors and therapists suggest that when couples falter in their communication, they begin to drift apart. According to the American Counseling Association, the common denominator in all failed marriages is a lack of communication.[2]

Just as poor communication sends a message to your business customers that you don't value them, lack of communication in your marriage gives your wife that same message. And as your wife observes you checking business email at home and texting customers at your daughter's concert, she begins to feel less and less important to you. And most of us guys get a little defensive if our wives gently suggest we turn off our Blackberries during dinnertime because, as we discussed earlier, the reason we work so hard is to provide for our loved ones.

Communication at home shouldn't be all that hard, so why is it cited so often as a major problem in so many marriages?

I'm not an expert, but I really think this is one of those cases in which a positive causes a negative. In my opinion, many good marriages tend to drift apart because they are such good marriages. Remember earlier when I mentioned how easy it is to ignore a customer when everything seems to be going well? I believe this is what happens to many good marriages. We get complacent. When we first began our courtship, we couldn't get enough communication and probably racked up hundreds of dollars in phone bills, back before unlimited billing plans. We looked for any occasion to buy a romantic greeting card and expressed our deepest thoughts and feelings to each other. Whether riding in the car or sitting over dessert in a restaurant, there were very few moments of silence.

Most men, according to conventional wisdom, are not really wired for so much conversation. I saw one report that the average woman speaks three times as many words a day as a man. I don't know if that's true or not, but in just my casual observations of men and women, I would have to agree that in general, we men do not talk all that much unless we're trying to close a deal or win over the love of our lives. Then we become chatterboxes. In marriage, once we settle into the rhythms of domestic bliss, we revert to our normal selves. It's not that we aren't interested in our wives or that they become less fascinating to us; we just don't see the need to spend as much time talking. It goes back to a positive turning into a negative. When you were trying to close a deal with a new client, you put your best communications skills to work. Once the client signed with your company and things got off to a great start, you didn't feel such a strong need to stay in touch. In other words, if a guy thinks things are going well, he's less likely to see the need for communication. "What's to talk about? We're doing okay, aren't we?"

Here's a sad but true story. An acquaintance was having lunch with a female colleague. As a man at another table got up to leave, he walked over to them and said, "You two can't be married to each other, because you've been talking the whole time you've been here." He probably meant it as a joke, but for this man—and probably for most American adults—married people just don't talk to each other that much.

But guess what? Both your highest performing customer and your wife and family *want* to hear from you. Often. Your customer expects ongoing communication because he's your client. You have a formal business relationship and he wants you to check in with him regularly. Your wife desires regular communication because she loves you. She cares about the things you care about and in a real sense wants to be your business partner, part of a team that will be together far longer than any business relationship at work.

Do What You Already Know

The good news is that you already know how to improve communication in your marriage. You do it every day at work. So let's look at how you can use what you already know to stay in touch with your team at home.

Perform a communications audit. Well-run businesses regularly review their communications, often paying a lot of money to consultants to perform this audit. They look at how information is communicated internally and externally; they interview employees, vendors, and customers; and then they give an extensive report card, grading the company on its efforts and suggesting ways to improve.

Not a bad idea for us to do at home. There's a tagline from a recent television commercial that explains why we need to do this: "Life comes at you fast." Perfect description for the world Charita and I live in, and I suspect it's the same for you. She has her social calendar and I have my business calendar and sometimes we're like two ships passing in the night. When we put it on autopilot like that, we usually experience a collision: she expects me to attend a community event with her, but I already have an important deadline and can't possibly join her. That's when we sit down to discuss what's going on in our two worlds and go over our "communications protocol." We don't call it that, but we had to have a little meeting and agree that before she puts something major on her calendar and before I add a commitment to my calendar, we need to check in with each other. Sounds really simple, but if we don't set aside some time regularly to take stock of how well we are staying in touch with each other despite our busy schedules, we tend to have too many of these conflicts, and that can be destructive.

Your communications audit doesn't have to be any more complicated than sitting down with your wife a couple of times a year and asking these questions:

- Do we set aside some time each day to touch base and at least look at our lives short-term?

- When one of us adds something to our calendar, do we make sure the other one gets the information?

- Do we always know how to reach each other when one of us travels?

- Do we have a regular time when we talk with each other about things that really matter to us, to get past the day-to-day stuff and share our thoughts about our lives, our faith, our dreams, our family?

- What grade would we give each other when it comes to communication?
- What could we do to improve?

If you take time to do this two or three times a year, you will be less likely to drift apart.

Establish a communications protocol. Smart businessmen establish a schedule for communicating with their valued customers. This is basically determining when and what type of communication is necessary to maintain a strong relationship, and to have some system to remind them to follow through. With your wife's input, establish a routine for staying in touch. It might look something like this:

- Daily

    A call home once during the day, if only to say hi
    Five minutes after supper to get caught up on the day's activities

- Weekly

    A review of the coming week every Sunday evening
    One-on-one with each child to stay involved in their lives

- Monthly

    Calendar check at Starbucks to coordinate business and family calendars
    Ticklers to remind you of anniversaries and birthdays

- Semiannually
    - Communications audit with your wife

Remember, the focus here is communication, not a schedule of all the fun activities you want to do with your wife and family. (That comes later.) As you can see, having a protocol doesn't add a lot of time to your busy lives, but the discipline to "follow protocol" will benefit you and your loved ones.

Take notes if you have to. One of the most common complaints of wives when it comes to communication is, "He just doesn't listen. I tell him things and it just goes in one ear and out the other. I swear he's thinking about a dozen things when I'm talking to him."

Truth? She's probably right. You probably *are* thinking about anything but what your wife is saying when you've carved out some time to talk. It is, to borrow a phrase, the nature of the beast when it comes to communication, and we struggle with it both in our careers and at home. But at work, we feel a greater urgency to pay attention and either take notes or, more likely, have an assistant not only take notes but promptly distribute them, highlighting action steps for everyone to follow through with.

I'm not really suggesting you take notes, but it might help. I know it sounds awfully formal, but why do you take notes in a meeting? Because you want to make sure you know what's going on and especially what you've been asked to do. Not a bad policy for when you're communicating with your wife and she asks you to pick up your daughter after gymnastics practice on Friday.

Don't just talk—connect. Have you ever sat through a presentation during which the presenter talked a lot but said very little? Or worse, he walked you through an elaborately designed PowerPoint presentation with thirty-seven slides and when he was finished you thought, "Now what was *that* all about?" It happens, and when it does, precious little communication is taking place. Sometimes we make the same mistake in our marriages. We think that because we're talking, we're communicating. We may be talking, but we're not connecting, and when that happens, it isn't long before no one's listening.

Here again is where you can put your business communications skills to work:

• *Make eye contact.* I know guys who can text while they talk to their wives. Not a good idea. You wouldn't think of doing that when you are talking to a customer. Pay attention when you and your wife are having a conversation. Engage her.

- *Ditch the monologue.* The best form of business communication is dialogue, give and take. When talking to your wife, pause occasionally to let her respond. Ask a question. Make it very clear that you want her input.

- *Step away from the podium.* Some men have this way of adopting a position of power or authority when they are talking to others. The "podium" in this case is a metaphor for anything you do to make your wife feel subservient. That can be anything from your posture (standing while she's sitting) to how loud you speak. Just because you're going over your calendars for the week doesn't mean you can't do it snuggled together on the couch. Be her partner, not her manager.

- *Lighten up.* Ever notice how so many people at work begin their presentations with a joke or a humorous story? Humor disarms people, helping them to connect better. I'm not saying you have to have a joke ready every time you talk to your wife, but you might need to lighten up, especially if you need to talk through a difficult situation: "Can you imagine us ever having a conversation like this when we were dating? We must be getting old and grumpy!"

Checking In

In the real world, even your best plans to maintain effective communication with your customers go awry. On paper, an effective communications strategy looks nice, but when things start to get a little crazy, you have to fly by the seat of your pants. One of the challenges in my business is that I have a lot of projects going on at once with a lot of customers whose needs are different. As an entrepreneur, I can't always schedule my life on a nine-to-five program. As opportunities present themselves, I need to move forward quickly. During these periodic "crash and burn" seasons, there's no way I can spend as much time communicating with each customer as I would like to. The temptation is just to let things go, but I have found a way to manage a frenzied schedule and still communicate regularly with my clients. I call it simply "the check-in," a quick phone call or an email just to see how things are going. I've learned that if I do this regularly, I'm able to stay in the game with my customers. They appreciate hearing from me, even if it's a two-minute call or a quick email. Plus, it keeps little problems from turning into expensive disasters.

I mention this because I know how things can get at home for you and I don't want to make it seem like you're a failure if you aren't sitting on the couch once a week with your wife going over your plans. Life is real and it's messy, and despite your good intentions, you're not always going to be able to enjoy great communication at home. As much as Charita and I would like to have those regular times to coordinate our calendars, we get so busy that we never quite know if we're coming or going. That's when "checking in" may be the best you can hope for. But you know what? That's not so bad. It's a whole lot better to check in, even briefly, than to let things build up to the point where you really have a breakdown in communication. Here's an example of what I mean:

It's late in Los Angeles. Your flight, scheduled to land at 8:00 p.m., touched down at eleven, and by the time you got to your hotel, it was past midnight. That's 2:00 a.m. back home. You always like to call your wife when you're out of town, but you're tired, she's probably asleep, and you just don't feel like talking anyway. This is the perfect occasion for checking in. Just a quick call to say, "I just got to the hotel. Just checking in on you guys. We can talk in the morning. I love you. Good night." Or if you don't want to wake her up but still want to check in, consider texting her. If she wakes up later and is worried about you, a quick check of her cell phone will reassure her.

The check-in is short and sweet, but it does two very important things. First, it reassures her and ends any worry she might have had in not hearing from you. Second, and maybe more important, it tells her she's important to you. Important enough to call even though you had one of those "flights from hell" type of travel days and just want to collapse on your bed.

It is often the little things we do that say the most and give us an A+ in communication: leaving a note on her pillow when you leave on a trip; calling when you leave the office to ask if she needs you to pick anything up on the way home; texting her from an important meeting she knows you stayed up late to prepare for; instead of heading home right after the movie, driving to your favorite park and inviting her to join you on a park bench, "Just to talk."

Given the fast-paced nature of our lives, we'll probably never reach our goals for communicating well with the ones we love the most. Things that shouldn't matter to us have a way of creeping into our lives and robbing us of the time we need to stay close and grow together. And the last thing you need is yet another list to check off, proving you're a great communicator.

So relax. Don't be too hard on yourself. Small improvements will come even if all you do is try to check in more often. You already use the skills and tools of a great communicator in your career; adapting them to use with those you love is not that difficult and eventually will come naturally.

6

Planning for
Great Outcomes

I HADN'T BEEN IN BUSINESS VERY LONG BEFORE I LEARNED ABOUT strategic planning. I can't say I sat down that first day I started an apparel business and began creating my strategic plan. I couldn't because I didn't know what a strategic plan was! I was running too fast, trying to stay ahead of the game. Order materials. Design the product. Find retailers to sell it for me. Pay the bills. And, I hoped, get paid by my retailers so I could stay in the black. But as my business grew, I realized I was heading for a train wreck if I didn't get a little more organized and develop a plan.

Strategic planning sometimes scares people off because it sounds complicated. Actually, strategic planning is pretty simple. It's a process for determining the direction a company is heading over a period of time (usually a year or more), identifying how it's going to get there, and perhaps most important, being able to know whether it has arrived. Strategic planning, then, involves a goal or vision, tactics, and measurement or evaluation.

When I first started in the apparel business, my goal was to survive, my tactics included working harder than anyone else, and I measured everything by whether I was still in business in a year. Once I saw that I was going to make it and got some experience under my belt, I began to be more strategic about my planning: how many new designs I would introduce; how many people I would need to hire; new sales channels I would develop; revenue and profit goals; efficiencies I would implement to reduce costs; standards for excellence and quality control.

While I have been blessed with a strong spirit of optimism—believing that just about everything is possible if you work hard enough—I have come to see that hard work isn't enough. But when you combine your strong work ethic with some consistent strategic planning, you have a much better chance of achieving your goals, professional or personal. Conversely, businesses that do not plan strategically almost always fail. I have seen one of the universal truths of the Bible proven in many businesses: without a vision, the people perish. Even talented individuals who start businesses with a great idea or product can find they eventually have to close up shop because they either had no strategic plan or failed to follow it. If you don't have a plan in place, then everyone is left to their own ideas and thoughts. The CFO may have one idea of where the company should be going, the sales team may have another idea, and the creative team may have yet another idea. They may all be good ideas, but strategically, it's not good for your company for everyone to be going in different directions. Without a clear plan that everyone understands, you end up wasting time and resources and ultimately you won't get the results you need to sustain your company.

Winging It in Marriage

A lot of us begin our marriages the way I started out in business: you just sort of go with the flow. You're in love, life seems pretty simple, and the thought of sitting down together to create a "strategic plan" almost feels like an intrusion into a great relationship:

"Sweetheart, our first weekend together as a married couple! Isn't it great? I love *you* and I love being married. What shall we do this weekend?"

"Um, I thought we'd get out our master calendars and develop a strategic plan for our lives."

I don't know about you, but that's not exactly how we spent our first weekend together as a married couple. And obviously, I'm not suggesting newlyweds need to set up a whiteboard as soon as they get back from the honeymoon. But it wasn't long before our lives did indeed get a little more complicated. We were both pursuing challenging careers, our circles of friends and influence widened, and the decisions we faced took on a seriousness that we hadn't experienced before as a couple. What about children? And if we start a family, what about our careers? What do we stand for as a couple? What do we stand against? Who's in charge of certain things, and what does that mean?

Like most couples, during those early years we winged it. I mean, we knew intuitively what each of us thought about these and other questions, and it's not like we never discussed them. But we never really sat down and systematically created a plan for our lives that would help us address the various situations that arise in any marriage. In our case, we were fortunate because whenever an opportunity or challenge came up, we seemed to already agree on the direction we should go, but for many couples, not being on the same page early in their marriages created insurmountable obstacles to a lasting relationship. Without a clear vision of what they expected of each other, they perished. For example, a Citicorp survey found that 57 percent of divorces stem from arguments over money.[3] Imagine how that number would go down if those couples had sat down and developed a plan for handling money.

Mickey and Ellen (not their real names) began arguing over money very soon after they got married. Mickey, who grew up in an affluent household, paid little attention to his spending habits. Ellen, who grew up in a household just above the poverty level, always shopped for bargains and tried to get Mickey to do the same. Soon, they found themselves overextended with credit card debt and arguing even more over what to do about it. Providentially, someone at their church told them about a seminar by debt guru Dave Ramsey.

A Template for a Simple Strategic Family Plan

Mission Statement

Our mission as a family is to _____

_____

_____

_____

The strengths that we want to emphasize and support in our family are

1. _____

2. _____

3. _____

The weaknesses that we want to work on correcting are

1. _____

2. _____

3. _____

Not only did they eventually get out of debt, the experience taught them how to develop a financial plan for their personal lives to ensure they didn't fall back into debt. Ironically, part of Mickey's job was to develop a financial plan for his department in his company, and

The opportunities available to us that we want to pursue are

1. _____

2. _____

3. _____

The threats to our family that we want to protect against are

1. _____

2. _____

3. _____

To help us achieve our mission, we will

1. _____

2. _____

3. _____

4. _____

he enjoyed the praise of his boss for keeping his department under budget. He had all the tools to stay out of debt at home, but he never thought of sharing those tools with his wife.

It may sound incongruous to apply strategic planning principles to your marriage, but if it's so important to success in the work world, shouldn't we treat our families at least as well as we treat our work? Strategic planning in marriage is as simple as identifying where you are headed as a family, how you plan to get there, and how you will know if you're successful. Most of us would agree on where we're headed when it comes to our spouses and families: we want thriving and long-lasting relationships. I'm guessing every marriage began with that goal, just as every business hopes to be profitable. But without a plan, as well as the discipline to follow it, review it regularly, and make adjustments when necessary, our goals become little more than wishful thinking.

Write the Vision

I wish I could say that once our space began to fill up and life became more complex, Charita and I sat right down and wrote out our strategic plan. We didn't. It wasn't until our kids were out of diapers that we got serious about living based on a plan we had created and therefore agreed with. To be honest, the motivation for developing our own strategic plan came from meeting with our attorney to draw up a will and create a trust for our kids. My attorney, who also happens to be my godfather and is a very wise man, said to me, "Louis, I want you to write a letter to your kids as if you were dying and would not be around for the rest of their lives. When you finish, I will be putting that with your will and trust documents so that your kids will know what their dad stood for, what he desired for them, and how he would have wanted them to live their lives."

Wow! Talk about a tough assignment. I went home that night

and sat down at my computer to write this letter, and within seconds I was out of control. I mean, I bawled like a baby as I was confronted with the possibility of my children going through life without me. Toughest letter I've ever written. But it also inspired me to go beyond this letter and spend some time with Charita really drilling down on who we are as a family, where we are going, what we hope to accomplish, and how we intend to live our lives.

It's probably not all that unusual for couples to talk about these things from time to time, but we decided to take it a step farther. Our inspiration came from ancient teaching in the Old Testament: "write the vision, and make it plain" (Habakkuk 2:2 KJV). We decided to write down our plan so that we have a record of it and can review it annually and, if necessary, amend it. In fact, I decided to treat our family the same way I would treat one of my clients, who frequently come to me and ask, "I need you to help us identify and communicate our brand," which is something I spend a lot of time doing. Novel idea, huh? Use what makes you a hero at work to be a hero to your family? But why not? Instead of jotting down a few things from our conversation about the future, I approached our life plan with the same professionalism I approach my most profitable customers' needs. I started just like I would in any branding meeting: what's our mission statement? Then with Charita's input, I began writing out our goals to guide us in trying to live out our mission statement. Then we worked on specific strategies — sort of the practical nuts and bolts of what we will or will not do as a family.

Being a designer at heart, I probably went a little farther than I would expect most couples to go — I designed a family crest. Actually, you don't need to be an artist to create a crest for your family. A crest is usually a few images or symbols that visually represent what matters most to you. Even if you don't actually create a family crest, it can be an interesting and instructive exercise to identify three or four images or objects that symbolize your values and beliefs.

Your Family Mission Statement

The key to any successful plan is to start with a mission or vision statement—a sentence or brief paragraph that defines goals, ambitions, standards, and so on. It provides any organization or individual a way to determine whether they are on course. One of the best ways to create a mission statement is to begin with a series of questions:

- What is our purpose as a family?
- What would we like our family to be remembered for?
- What would we like to be our legacy?
- What adjectives would best describe our family?
- What contributions do we want to make to our neighborhood, our society?
- What are the top two or three character traits that we covet for ourselves and our children?
- What do we stand for? What would we be willing to die for?

Companies that develop mission statements for the first time discover that it takes time, so don't expect to create your family mission statement in an evening. Also, don't try to do it by yourself. Successful mission statements aren't handed down from one person but are the result of vigorous collaboration. A good way to start after you go through your list of questions is for both you and your wife to write a first draft of a mission statement, compare them, and then start over as a team to write the second draft. It may take several drafts before you both agree that you have captured exactly what you desire for each other and your family, so stick with it.

Here are some sample family mission statements to get you started.

- Our mission is to become a source of encouragement and inspiration to our community. We will seek opportunities to volunteer and therefore demonstrate by our actions the gospel that we believe in and that guides us in all we do.

- Our mission is to be leaders rather than followers. We will strive in our work, at school, and at home to excel so that our example compels others to follow and therefore contribute to a better society.

- Our mission as a family is to put God and his teachings ahead of anything else. We want to be known as humble followers of Christ at work, at home, at school, and at play.

- We will be a family that is known for its love and compassion. We will treat each other lovingly, even when we disagree. And we will attempt to live out this mission in our various circles of influence so that people will say of us, "How they love one another."

Mission statements, like family plans, are dynamic. They need to be reviewed at least once a year, for two purposes. First, to evaluate your performance, to see how well you are fulfilling your mission. And second, to see if your mission statement needs to be adjusted to meet your family's changing needs.

Taking SWOT Home

If you work in a business that does strategic planning, you've probably heard about SWOT so much that you can recite the acronym in your sleep: strengths, weaknesses, opportunities, threats. Practically every strategic planning session in business begins with a SWOT analysis. This term, hardly new, was coined in the 1960s by Albert Humphrey, who was leading a research project at Stanford University involving Fortune 500 companies. The fact that it is still used today speaks for its value and, in my opinion, suggests it might also be helpful to families.

What I like about using SWOT for your family's strategic plan is that it is simple yet focuses on areas that critically affect the overall health of your marriage and family relationships. For example, if I asked you to list three or four strengths in your marriage, would you have a ready answer? And would your spouse answer the same way? Most people I know would have difficulty, initially, listing the strong points of their marriage and need some time to think about it. That's not necessarily a bad thing; it only underscores the value of carving out some time with your spouse to go through a SWOT analysis.

As I said, the SWOT analysis is pretty simple, but just as any business must determine how to implement it, you will need to be sure to apply it to your family. While there is no right or wrong way to conduct a SWOT analysis at home, I recommend you try doing what is pretty common in businesses and other organizations: schedule a planning retreat. Find a day or weekend when you can get away from your routines and mix a little business and pleasure. If that's not possible, then set aside one evening a week to work through each of its components. That way, within one month you will have completed the exercise.

Also, a little structure will help you and your spouse identify specific answers for each of the components. Here are some questions and suggestions to guide you through each area of the SWOT analysis.

Strengths

1. As individuals, what are our strengths? What strengths do each of us bring into our relationships? (For example, I'm a detail person; I'm tenacious and have a never-give-up attitude; I can do several things at once; I'm an optimist.)

2. How do our individual strengths complement each other?

3. As a married couple, what are our strengths? (For example, we share the same basic beliefs; we communicate well and

regularly with each other; we are extremely loyal to each other.)

Weaknesses

1. As individuals, what are our weaknesses? What weaknesses do each of us bring into our relationships? (For example, I am a procrastinator; I have a quick temper; I'm lousy at handling money.)

2. How do our individual weaknesses affect our relationship?

3. As a married couple, what are our weaknesses? (For example, we let little disagreements turn into arguments; we spend too much time with our kids and not with each other; we have very few friendships with other couples.)

Opportunities

1. As individuals, what opportunities or new possibilities exist for each of us — good things to look forward to? (For example, a new job; additional education or training; volunteering; hobbies; reunion with old friends.)

2. If we pursue these individual opportunities, how will it affect our relationship?

3. As a married couple, what opportunities or new possibilities exist for us — good things we can look forward to? (For example, purchase a new house; a major home improvement project; a vacation; our daughter's graduation.)

Threats

1. As individuals, where are we vulnerable? What potential problems face each of us? (For example, I could become a workaholic; I'm really lonely and don't have any close friends; I tend to drink too much when I am under a lot of stress; I'm feeling a little resentful that I put my career on hold.)

2. How can we help protect each other from these individual threats?

3. As a married couple, what threatens our relationship? Where are we vulnerable to forces or events that could push us apart? (For example, we are both way too busy; we do not have other couples to share our lives with; we are going through some severe financial stress.)

As you go through this process, avoid the temptation to take charge or to challenge any of your wife's answers or statements. This is really an opportunity for you to grow in your knowledge of each other as you prepare to create a plan that will keep your marriage healthy and strengthen your family. Make it fun, an adventure of discovery. What you are really doing is creating a snapshot of your marriage to help you build on what's good and protect yourselves from what's not so good.

Create Your Plan

Writing your mission statement and going through the SWOT analysis provides you with some baseline information for creating a strategic plan for your family. Now it's time to dig in and put together a plan. How are you going to get from where you are right now to a place where you can say you are living up to your mission statement? What sorts of activities and experiences need to take place on a regular basis? What are some objectives that will help you reach your goal?

Someone whose example has really encouraged me to engage in strategic planning for my family is Kemmons Wilson, Chairman of the Board for Wilson Hotel Management, a very successful business that manages Holiday Inn hotels and motels. Kemmons, whose father founded the Holiday Inn chain and instilled great values in his son, has been very intentional about planning for his family. Having seen the pitfalls of sons and daughters being given jobs in the family business, he developed a career plan for his children. It was pretty specific. Instead of getting a job in their dad's company when they got out of college, they had to go out on their own and find a job; they had to achieve success in an environment where no one could accuse them of getting favorable treatment, and only then could they

Goal-Setting for Families

Most people make the mistake of setting goals that are too broad, ambitious, or vague. I call those "feel-good goals." They sound nice, but they are not very effective because you have no way of knowing your progress toward meeting them. Your goal-setting will be more effective if you develop "action-oriented goals." An action-oriented goal will have most of the following characteristics:

1. *Focused.* You know exactly where you are heading because your goal is specific.

2. *Measurable.* You know when you are getting close and when you have arrived.

3. *Achievable.* It is realistic and can be attained with appropriate action.

4. *Significant.* Realizing this goal will have a major impact on your family.

Feel-good goal: "We will strive to grow spiritually."

Action-oriented goal: "We will spend ten minutes each day reading the Bible and praying and listening to God."

enter the family business. Kemmons' plan for his children included having them become respected and to develop self-confidence, and he knew if they were given jobs in his business right out of college, they might not have either.

When Kemmons shared this with me, I thought, "Wow! What a great gift he's giving his family." And that's what planning can do. Great CEOs and managers do their employees and customers a huge favor when they unleash their best thinking and creativity to do strategic planning, and I want to do the same thing for the people I love the most. I know you do too, but it feels a little foreign to us. Where do I start? How detailed should it be? What if I miss something that should be included? All good questions, but for now, relax. Even a modest plan will be a step in the right direction and will be better than no plan at all.

Start with your mission statement and try to identify at least one objective or action step that will move you toward that mission. For example, let's say your mission identified "taking care of creation" as something your family wants to address. Here's how that part of your plan might look.

- We will recycle as much of our waste as possible.
- We will replace at least ten lightbulbs with energy efficient bulbs.
- We will turn off computers and video games when we are not using them.
- We will volunteer as a family at least twice a year to pick up trash for the Adopt a Highway program.

Your family plan can be this simple—a few clearly stated objectives to guide your actions. In fact, if you've never had a family plan, I recommend starting out small and simple, with something that is doable and allows your family to celebrate its success. The great thing about writing out your good intentions is that what you've written becomes a benchmark against which to measure your progress. If you can put your mission statement and plan on a single sheet of paper, it makes a great document to display prominently in your home, such as on the refrigerator or on a family bulletin board, providing a daily reminder to everyone that this is who you want to be.

Keeping Your Dreams Alive

As a dad, I have big dreams for my wife and my children. I'm sure you do too. I'm sure all of us at one time had hopes that our son or daughter would become president (or an astronaut or someone who discovers the cure for cancer), but what did we do to encourage that to happen? That's why I'm sold on developing a master plan for my family. I truly believe that my wife and my children have so much to offer this world to make it a better place, but unless we plan for that outcome, we might all miss opportunities to excel and contribute.

Developing a business plan at work gives my company two things: purpose and hope. Purpose in that we know what we are doing and why. And a very real hope that we can be successful. Imagine the benefits for your family if you used this skill which is practically second nature for you at work. It's so easy for us in our families to let activities crowd out any sense of purpose, but if you take the time to step out of the rat race and with your wife work through a strategic plan for your family, you will give those dreams for the people you love the most a chance to blossom.

Finally, developing a plan for your family will help clear out a lot of the clutter in your lives because it gives you something to focus on rather than chasing everything that comes your way. Most of us are blessed with so many great opportunities, but without some standard to evaluate them by, many of these good things that we're doing are actually distractions. Even a simple plan like the one outlined above gives you permission to say no to a lot of stuff. It's what we do at work all the time. Someone comes to me with a great idea, and it might even be one that could make a lot of money for the company, but when I measure it against our mission statement and business plan, it becomes clear that this is something that will not take us closer to our mission. One of the most common complaints I hear from so many of my friends is that their family lives are practically chaotic because they are filled with so many good activities. If that sounds like you, there's yet another reason to schedule that planning retreat with your wife so that you can begin living with purpose.

7

Your Word
Is Your Bond

Here's an assignment for you. When you go to work tomorrow, find a way to cheat one of your best customers. If you're a salesman, overcharge your best client. If you're a lawyer, leak some privileged information about your top client to the media. If you manage someone's investments, skim a little off his profit and into your own pockets.

Pretty absurd, right? Cheating your customer is a good way to lose that customer, get fired, or land in jail. Or all three. Recent news of high-level scandals in business notwithstanding, you simply cannot be successful in your work if you cheat. At least not for very long. Eventually, dishonesty catches up with you, and when it does the results are disastrous. Whatever reputation you have earned in your line of work, one slip in the area of integrity and you can spend the rest of your career trying to repair the damage. And because your behavior is a reflection on the company you represent, responsible businesses expect you to be honest and trustworthy, often spelling this out in ethics policies. Type in the words "ethics policies for employees" in any search engine, and you'll find more than six million entries, and the majority of them are ethics policies for individual businesses.

I understand the need to conduct my business with the highest level of integrity, and the following two stories illustrate the challenges this presents.

I received a letter a while back from a woman I hadn't seen for more than seven years. Right out of nowhere, this letter arrives, and as I read it, I learned that she had seen me on television and wrote to compliment me—at least that was the stated reason for her letter. But as I read on, my heart almost stopped. She went on to say that a mutual friend of ours had also seen me on television and had a different reaction. This other person was a professional seamstress with whom I had done some business, and as the two of them talked about seeing me on television, the seamstress mentioned that she had never been paid for a job she did for me. Wow! My first reaction was to be thankful that this woman mentioned my apparent failure in her letter. I vividly recalled the work the seamstress did for me and it pained me to think that for more than a year she thought of me as a cheat. What if I had never gotten this letter? It sent a chill through my heart to think of how much more damage could have been done if over the years the seamstress mentioned this to others.

My next reaction was to dig out our billing statements to see what had happened. From day one, I have always believed that you pay your bills on time, and I couldn't imagine I let this fall through the cracks. As it turned out, we had indeed cut a check and sent it to her. Puzzled, I investigated further and learned that the building where the woman had her business had been demolished. In a freak set of circumstances, we sent her check to that address, which at the time was a pile of bricks and wood; the check was never returned to our offices, nor was it forwarded to her new business. Shame on us for not noticing that the check had never been cashed, but it was for a relatively small amount of money—three hundred dollars—so it didn't catch anyone's attention. An honest mistake, but one I *had* to make right.

I immediately called the woman and apologized, offering to hand deliver the check that day.

"You don't have to do that, Louis," she replied.

"No, I insist — this is very important to me."

Finally she relented, but then I asked her why she never called to let me know she had never gotten the check.

"Oh, I just didn't want to make a big deal about it."

I learned a couple of important lessons from this incident. First, we may not always know when we have disappointed others, which underscores the importance of paying close attention to issues of integrity. And second, loss of integrity has no price tag. Even though this was a relatively small amount of money, the effect was the same as if I had owed her three thousand dollars. When I discovered that I owed her only three hundred, I could have just blown it off because it wasn't much money. But to her, it wasn't a small amount. By taking the time to discover what had happened, I was able to restore my reputation with her.

The second story happened in the early years of our company and has to do with a potential customer who approached me with a project that was almost irresistible. It was exciting, it would allow us to do what we do best in a richly creative environment, and it would pay well. Extremely well. As an independent businessman, you look for these opportunities, and I was right at the end of the diving board. As we were evaluating the deal, I drilled down a little more with this potential customer to get a better idea of the creative side of the project and immediately knew I had to say no. I learned that we would be creating T-shirts for a notoriously foul-mouthed rapper, and some of the content that would be on the T-shirts violated my principles. At the time, I was spending many of my weekends going to the housing projects to work with young kids there and try to instill in them the values of life as a Christian. Yes, the money was good, but I wasn't about to use my talents to get this type of product in the marketplace and risk my reputation just to make money. Sure, probably no one ever would have known I designed these shirts, because our company name would not appear on them. But I would know. My conscience told me that if I rationalized my way into this deal, there would be others like it to follow and it wouldn't be long before I became the very person I had built my career trying to avoid. It reminded me of the values our business stood for and the promise I made to myself to avoid working with the type of client I was about to shake hands with. It practically shouted, "Don't do it, Louis! No amount of money is worth losing your reputation."

I backed away from the deal.

I share these two stories to show how in our careers, integrity is not just a fancy word but something we need to work at and integrate into practically every decision we make. More important, it is something so vital that we are willing to go the extra mile to protect our good reputations. I'm sure you could also tell stories of being tempted to cut ethical corners and choosing instead to take the high road.

So here's my question: are you as careful with your word around your spouse as you are with your customers and colleagues?

Full Disclosure

It was one of those beautiful fall days we have here in Nashville. I had just parked my car and was heading into my office when I got a text message from someone whose name was vaguely familiar: "Hi Louis. Call when u can. 615.555.5555. Denise W." Before responding, I racked my brain to try to figure out who this woman was. Obviously she knew me. And from the area code I knew she must be local. I mouthed the name a couple of times and then I called the number. I learned Denise was a girl I had dated in college, some seventeen years ago. It turned out she had her own business and was looking to add new clients. Perfectly legitimate and on the up and up, she had gotten my number from a mutual friend who couldn't have known we once dated. Her business wasn't really a good match with mine, so I politely declined and that was that—no, "We ought to get together and get caught up," or any questions outside of business. As far as I know, this was an enterprising woman trying to grow her business, just another blip on my daily calendar.

But it wasn't. It was a former girlfriend. True, we had only dated casually for about three months. And that was seventeen *years* ago. But if my wife discovered from anyone else but me that I had spoken with an ex-girlfriend, I would at least have a little explaining to do, and no matter how carefully I explained, this "insignificant" event would have understandably raised a sliver of doubt in Charita's mind. "Hmm. I wonder why he didn't want to tell me about the call?"

Many businesses believe so strongly in full disclosure that they publish formal statements to guide their employees' behavior: "___ believes that full disclosure in any business relationship is characterized by both parties having full and equal access to all information relevant and necessary to maintaining an equitable business relationship. This means that both sides of that relationship have full confidence in each other's integrity and commitment to share any and all information that directly or indirectly impacts the other party."

This statement, from a prominent business in the health-care industry, represents a growing trend in business to be as open as possible with partners and clients. What stood out to me in this company's statement were the words "full confidence in each other's integrity." It sounds exactly like what should be the norm for marriages, but sadly, I run into a lot of guys who feel it's okay to keep things from their wives.

A friend of mine tells of joining four other guys for dinner at a nice restaurant to celebrate one of the younger men's impending marriage. All but the bachelor were happily married, representing a total of sixty-four years of marriage. Someone suggested it would be nice if they went around the table and gave advice to their single friend about the intricacies of marriage. "We covered the usual stuff, but I was taken aback by one guy's comment," my friend recounted. "He actually advised our buddy not to tell his wife everything, because some things are just better kept secret. This guy was an elder in his church and highly respected in the community."

I can't think of worse advice to give a man about to be married. Sooner or later, our secrets get out, and when that happens in a marriage, it totally destroys trust. Which is why, as soon as I hung up the

Becoming a Man of Integrity

Thanks to our human nature and temptation from the Enemy, you never fully arrive when it comes to integrity. It's something we need to pay attention to every day. The minute you think you're beyond temptation, you've opened the door to a lapse in integrity. Over the years, I have worked hard to be a man of integrity, and I'm still learning. Here are some things that have helped me along the way.

1. *Develop and maintain a strong relationship with God.* For me this means being part of a dynamic church where I can worship regularly with others, spending time daily in prayer and studying the Bible, and being obedient to the teachings of Jesus.

2. *Seek relationships with mentors.* The wisdom and experience of older men helps keep me grounded and encourages me to follow their examples.

3. *Form an accountability partnership.* I have a couple of guys about my age I meet with regularly and can be honest and

phone with my former girlfriend, I dialed my wife and told her about the call, recounting it practically word for word. I wanted her to hear about this call from me and no one else. And I wanted her to know that I didn't hesitate to tell her about it so that she would know I didn't even have to think twice about being forthright with her. The longer you wait to do the right thing, the harder it is to actually do it. If I had waited to tell her later in the day, here's the conversation I might have had with myself: "I can't really tell her now because she'll ask me why I didn't tell her the instant it happened. Gee, I wish I had told her this morning. I sure don't want to make her suspicious and

open with about any area of my life. We hold each other accountable.

4. *Avoid putting yourself in danger.* This includes everything from the websites you visit on the internet to going into a bar alone at night to the kinds of entertainment you seek.

5. *Confess early and often.* We all make mistakes, but the biggest mistake is trying to cover them up. Integrity means no secrets, so don't keep any.

6. *Be who you are, all the time.* Are you the same person at home as you are at work? At church? Strive to be the same person all the time.

7. *Invest in your family.* The more involved you are in your wife's life and the lives of your children, the more you will want to be a husband and father of integrity. They are great motivators for you to be true to your word.

think I was trying to decide whether to tell her. Maybe just this once I'll just keep a secret from her."

"Just this once" has done a lot of guys in when it comes to honesty in marriage. It usually begins with a very small matter: "Did you remember to call the school?" or, "You mailed the bills yesterday, didn't you?"

Maybe you forgot to call the school, but you don't want to admit it, and besides, you'll call them tomorrow and no one will know the difference. It's that kind of thinking that gradually erodes your conviction to be a man of your word and paves the way for being untruthful about bigger things. I don't think any man starts out in his marriage with any intention to be untruthful, but to avoid conflict, he occasionally takes shortcuts around the truth. Once that begins, each shortcut becomes easier and easier. The obvious solution is just not to take any shortcuts when it comes to integrity, but that's easier said than done. Here are some ways you can consistently be a man of your word at home just as you seek to do that at work.

Find an accountability partner. One of the best ways to preserve your integrity is to have a trusted friend or small group of friends with whom you can share your deepest thoughts and struggles. If you give this person permission to ask you anything, he can help keep you honest at work and at home. Tell him that you want to be held accountable for issues of trust and truthfulness with your wife and children, and don't get defensive if he follows through with some tough questions.

When I was a younger man, I really struggled with lust, and there was this one woman whose very voice was enough to drive me crazy. I've never done drugs, but she was my cocaine. I was also digging deep to be a true man of God, so whenever she called and left a message on my phone, I would delete it so that I wouldn't have her number and therefore wouldn't be able to call her back. I remember sharing my struggle with a small group of men I met with each week as we encouraged each other to live godly lives, and that very night when I got back to my apartment, her voice was on my answering machine. This time, however, I didn't delete her message, and that scared me. Quickly, I dialed one of the guys in my group and told him what happened, and then said, "Here's what you've gotta do for me. I want you to stay on the phone and talk to me until I fall asleep or I might go ahead and call her." I called him at 9:00 p.m. and he stayed on the phone with me until 3:00 a.m.! I know that sounds crazy and funny, but it was so important to me at the time to rid myself of something that wasn't good for me. Thankfully, I had someone to call and had enough courage to open up my world for him to see exactly who I was and to help me. He also offered a little friendly advice right up front: "Louis, delete her message. Now!"

I share this story because that long phone call broke the spell this woman had on me, and I was never again tempted to have anything to do with her. We really need to find a handful of men who love the Lord and with whom we can be real. Today, we laugh about that phone call, but at the time I really believed my moral integrity was at stake.

Be careful about your promises. Some men have the best of intentions and promise things to their wives or children that they cannot realistically deliver. When that happens, it erodes trust. If you promise your daughter to take her to get ice cream after school on Friday and then tell her Friday morning that you can't make it because of a late meeting at work, she translates that as, "I can't trust my dad," or worse, "My dad is always lying to me." Promise only what you know you can deliver.

Don't let the sun go down on a lie. Well, the actual verse from the Bible is a good one: "do not let the sun go down while you are still angry" (Ephesians 4:26). But I think it's a good practice for truthfulness too. End each day by reviewing with your wife your "truthfulness inventory." If you shaded the truth even a little that day but set the record straight at night, you will have a clean slate by the end of every day. Even if you're just tempted to cover something up, tell her. The more she sees you really working at being a man of integrity, the more she will trust you.

Keep all accounts open. Your wife should have access to all your email accounts, financial accounts, passwords, and so on. No secrets. (The only exception might be if you are a pastor or counselor and have to maintain standards of confidentiality with your parishioners or clients, but you can still give your wife access to your *personal* accounts.) This is a big one because our computers provide us with a lot of opportunities to hide things. She should be able to read any email you get and go to any website you've visited. This not only gives her greater trust in you, it causes you to think twice about doing anything with these accounts that you wouldn't want her to know about.

Build walls of protection around you. One reason men lie is that they want to cover up behavior that they know would disappoint their wives. So it goes without saying that you should avoid any activity that you wouldn't want her to find out about. I love the warning printed on the masthead of the *Aspen Daily News*: "If you don't want it printed, don't let it happen." Stay away from the things you know you should stay away from, and then you won't feel the need to hide anything. If you have a problem with alcohol, stay away from bars. If you struggle with pornography, set the parental controls on your computer to filter the bad stuff. (I know of a man who when he checks into a hotel on a business trip asks the front desk to block his TV from receiving adult movies—smart guy.)

Confess immediately. No one's perfect. If you tell even a "little white lie," confess it as soon as you can. The longer you put off coming clean to your wife when you've been untruthful, the worse it gets. For one thing, it will become harder and harder to make it right. And your wife will wonder why it took you so long. She knows you'll make mistakes and will respect you if you take care of them sooner rather than later.

Lost Trust Regained

I was talking with a man recently who had violated his wife's trust a number of times. He knew what he did was wrong and he confessed everything to his wife, who was generous with her forgiveness. But his question is one that I suspect a lot of men might ask: "Will my wife ever be able to trust me again?" This is a tough one, because every person is different. But here again is where you might draw on your experience in the workplace.

Let's say you promised one of your key customers that you would deliver a big order on a particular date, but you were unable to make the deadline. Further, this customer needed that order so that his sales wouldn't suffer. Not getting it meant he lost of a lot of revenue. Aside from being very upset with you, he probably wouldn't be interested in doing business with you again. But you really want to keep him as a customer. What would you do? I don't know the specifics of what you would do, but it would look something like this: whatever it takes! Here are some suggestions to help you regain the trust that you lost with your wife.

Apologize and accept responsibility. Your wife will be less likely to trust you if you try to blame others or circumstances. The first step in regaining trust is to acknowledge what you did and apologize. Sounds simple, but so many people try to rationalize or explain away their behavior rather than just "fess up" and apologize.

Deal with your problem. Why did you feel the need to lie or otherwise act in a way that was untrustworthy? Usually it's to cover up some kind of behavior that you know is wrong or at least is unacceptable in a relationship. Whatever it is, turn away from it. If it's an addiction, such as to pornography or gambling, get help. No matter how much you apologize, if you continue the behavior, you will most likely continue to try to cover it up. Most wives want to walk through the valley with their husbands as long as they believe he is making an honest effort to turn things around.

Accept anger or disappointment without complaining or getting defensive. Your wife may be very upset with you for lying or otherwise violating her trust. That's normal, and you will begin to gain her confidence if you are understanding and patient. Don't pressure her to get over it or get upset with her if she continues to express her disappointment with you. Suck it up and adopt a biblical strategy that will eventually disarm that anger: "A gentle answer turns away wrath, but a harsh word stirs up anger" (Proverbs 15:1).

Show her you understand why she is mistrusting. Because you violated her trust, she may feel the need to quiz you more than usual or

Pause for a Moment

Psychologists explain that sometimes people lie because they want to please others. So instead of answering a question honestly, they try to answer in a way that would please the other person. For example, a customer asks if you can give him free shipping. Or you walk in the door after a long day at work and your daughter asks you, "Daddy, can we go to the movies Saturday afternoon?" Because you want to please both your customer and your daughter, you might say, "Sure!" without really thinking about whether you can deliver. So when I get questions like that, I say something like, "I'd love to, but let me think about it first to make sure I can." Taking that little pause brings me back to earth, allowing me to give a promise I can fulfill.

scrutinize your actions. If that happens, provide her with any information she requests and do it with a loving heart. This is really a favor to you because it gives you a chance to show her she can ask you anything and not worry about your getting upset. The more open you are with her when she asks these questions, the more likely it will be that she will begin to trust you again.

Let time heal your wounds. Depending on the seriousness of the breach of trust, it could take several months before your wife feels she can trust you again. Maybe years. Trust is a precious commodity that takes years to gain and can be lost with one foolish mistake. Time is your friend, so allow your wife as much time as she needs to reach a point where she can fully trust you.

Let your actions speak. If your word has been compromised with your wife, the only language she will trust for a while will be your actions. Don't tell her you love her—show her. Don't tell her she can trust you—show her. What you do will have more influence on her than what you say. If you consistently "walk the talk," you will earn back her trust and respect.

The Daily Grind

Integrity, whether at work or at home, is not the sort of thing you work on every now and then. You don't set aside one day a month to work on your integrity much like you might pay your bills. It's something we have to address almost 24/7 because of the insidious nature of dishonesty, which always presents us with small, seemingly insignificant openings. Few people actually decide to outright lie or cheat; rather, they find themselves taking shortcuts out of convenience. I read somewhere that according to a company that conducted 3.8 million background checks on people applying for jobs, more than half lied on their resumes.[4] These aren't horrible people or chronic liars but ordinary citizens like you and me who think those little white lies are okay and will never be caught anyway. Unfortunately, even if they are never caught, they erode our standards and make it easier to make duplicity the norm.

In 1912, Leon Leonwood Bean started a mail order business in Greenwood, Maine, by selling a hunting boot with a money-back guarantee. However, defects in the design led to 90 percent of them being returned. Making good on the guarantee could ruin his fledgling business, but Leon kept his word, corrected the design, and continued selling the boots. L.L. Bean is now one of the largest mail-order companies in the United States, in large part because it has continued the tradition of treating its customers with integrity.

Being a man of your word is not always easy, and like Leon Bean, you will make mistakes along the way. But if you treat your wife and loved ones the way Mr. Bean treated his customers, you will enjoy a long and fruitful relationship with them as they realize that you love them enough to be exactly who you are even when no one is watching.

8

World-Class
Customer Service

I'M A BIG PROPONENT OF CUSTOMER SERVICE, BOTH AS A CONSUMER and as a businessman. As a consumer, I'm even willing to pay more for a product if the people selling it treat me well. And as a businessman, I know that my success depends not only on the quality of the product I provide but also on the level of service I give my customers. World-class customer service is one of those things in business that doesn't really cost anything until you quit delivering it, and then it can cost you a lot. Smiling at a customer when she pays her bill costs the same as frowning, but keep frowning and you'll begin to lose customers. When it comes to customer service, it's usually the little things that count.

Although I fly most of the major airlines, my favorite in terms of customer service is Southwest. They seem to understand that even the worst travel experiences can be remedied simply by treating each customer respectfully. Perhaps the best example of that was reported a few years ago in *Business Week*. Apparently, one of Southwest's flights got caught in those weather delays that can stretch on forever. After sitting on the ground in snowy conditions and having to be de-iced twice, the plane was just about to take off when the pilot reached his shift deadline set by the Federal Aviation Administration, sending the plane back to the gate to await a new pilot. Even though the plane was delayed a total of five hours, few passengers complained and most had nothing but good things to say about the airline. Why? Because during the delay the pilot himself walked the aisles, greeting the passengers and giving them updates about the weather and their connections, and basically shared the delay with them. Then, within a couple of days after the flight, each passenger received two free round-trip travel vouchers.

If you travel as much as I do, you know that this just doesn't happen on other airlines. You're lucky to get a muffled sentence or two from the pilot over the PA system. If you ask about your connection, you might get a shrug from a flight attendant. It didn't cost Southwest an extra penny for the pilot to mingle with the passengers and reassure them, and those free travel vouchers only guaranteed that a hundred or so passengers would make Southwest their carrier of choice.

In my experience as a businessman, I've found that even the simplest customer-service skills ensure long-term loyalty from your customers. Things like:

- Returning calls promptly
- Seeing every interaction with them as an opportunity to win them over with kindness, friendliness, and politeness (never taking them for granted)
- Treating them as if they are more important to you than you are to them
- Using customers' names when you talk to them
- Listening carefully to your customers when they talk to you and looking them in the eyes so they know you care about what they are saying
- Following through with what you say you will do

- Showing empathy and understanding their needs rather than assuming you know their needs
- Receiving their complaints without defensiveness and quickly addressing them
- Turning off the cell phone when meeting with a customer
- Looking for ways to compliment the customer
- Going the extra mile whenever possible

If you're like me, you do a pretty good job on these things. Your customer might be your boss or a colleague or a vendor, but you've perfected the art of treating the people you interact with at work in a way that makes them enjoy being around you. But here's the tough part: how often do you practice these basic customer-service skills with the person you're in love with?

The Customer You Sleep With

If you're a little embarrassed to answer that question truthfully, I'll let you off the hook and answer it myself: not nearly as much as I ought to. While I pride myself in giving my customers great customer service, I'll admit I don't always turn off my cell phone when I'm talking to my wife, and I've also been guilty of not paying close attention to her when she's talking to me. Which is silly, when you stop to think about it. I mean, I love my customers, and without them I wouldn't have much of a business. But I don't live with them. They aren't helping me raise my children. They haven't nursed me back to health when I was sick, nor have they had to put up with me when I'm in a bad mood. They always get to view me at my best, while my wife is one of the few people to see me at my very worst. They get to meet with me in nice restaurants or in comfortable boardrooms, while sometimes Charita gets only a few seconds while I'm shaving in front of the mirror in my boxers. Naturally, my customers like me because I work hard to please them; it's a miracle, some days, that my wife still likes me, because I give so much to my customers that there's little left over for her. Yet she not only still likes me but loves me as well. Why *shouldn't* she get my best customer service?

The best way I can answer that is to fall back on our human nature. Typically, the best customer service occurs at the beginning of a business relationship. You're in that courtship phase when you want to showcase the best you can offer in order to gain a new cus-

Dress for Success

One of the "softer" forms of customer service is your appearance. When you meet with clients, you pay attention to the way you look and how you present yourself. It's just another way to show them how important they are to you. And while it's fine to relax when you get home, consider what your appearance communicates to your wife and family. It's one thing to put on an old pair of jeans and a T-shirt to mow the lawn. In fact, many of our wives love to see us in our old T's and a raggedy pair of jeans because it reminds them of a time when we were a lot more carefree. But when you come in for dinner, what's so hard about at least taking a shower and changing into some clean clothes? I'm not talking about dressing up; I'm talking about just taking the time to be a little more presentable. And even if you're only taking the family out to McDonald's, do you really want them to walk in with a slob? Here's a good rule to follow: anytime you engage in a planned activity outside of your home with your wife or family, treat it as if you were meeting with a key client or colleague.

tomer. Once you win over that customer, the challenge is to continue delivering world-class service. At some point, you begin to think that customer will always be with you, and that's when you inadvertently start cutting corners. It's not that you don't value this customer—you do. But you don't make the same effort to show that customer that you value them. Unless you make customer service a priority, this pattern is inevitable, and it's exactly what happens in most marriages.

Think back on all the little (and big) customer-service strategies you used when you were dating your wife. When did you begin slacking off on these strategies, and why? Chances are, within the first year or two of your wedding day, you both began settling into routines that made those caring acts seem either impossible or unnecessary. For example, before you were married, you probably did your best to show up for a date well groomed, well dressed, and maybe with a little gift. Now that you wake up beside her every morning, it's impractical to hop up to go comb your hair and brush your teeth and bring her a box of chocolates. Being married and living together poses challenges that your customers never have to deal with, so we need to be a little realistic with ourselves and realize that marriage is a 24/7 deal. You can't be "on" every second you're with your wife and family as you are with a customer.

Taking Customer Service Home with You

On the other hand, we can't let familiarity become an excuse for ignoring the needs of our loved ones. Just because you live together, sleep together, and do a lot of other things together doesn't mean you are showing your wife that she is more important than any customer. Basically, customer service is anything that demonstrates to the customer one vital message: you are important to me. Without realizing it, we often do things in our relationships that tell our wives, "You're not really that important to me."

For example, during the first Christmas Charita and I spent together as a married couple, I shopped for her present the way I always shop: mentally. I know lots of you are probably saying, "That's not very smart, Louis." I know. But I *do* spend a lot of time thinking about what to get her; it's just that for the actual purchasing, I head to the mall late in the day on December 24. Unfortunately, as I was leaving the mall with the gift I had purchased, our local television station had their camera and a reporter waiting at the exit to interview last-minute shoppers, and sure enough, he interviewed me. And Charita was watching at that very moment! When I got home, she was upset and told me that by waiting until the last minute to buy her a Christmas gift, it made her feel like an afterthought—not very important to me. Of course I explained how I had put a great deal of thought into her gift, but to her, my actions spoke louder than my words. It was a little thing, really, but it sent the wrong message.

Experiences like that have taught me that you don't have to take exceptional measures to give your loved ones great customer service. Just pay attention to the way you serve your customers. Imagine what would happen if you took the list of "little things" I previously mentioned and made them a priority with your wife and family:

Returning calls promptly. If my assistant comes into my office and tells me one of my customers called while I was in a meeting and wants me to call her back, I respond immediately and make the call. I also try to do that when my wife calls. I've been told by her and other women that nothing frustrates them more than not being able to reach their husbands at work. It makes them feel like they really don't matter very much, especially if an assistant is screening your calls.

Seeing every interaction with them as an opportunity to win them over with kindness, friendliness, and politeness (never taking them for granted). Just be nice. Yes, there will be times when you're grumpy or overstressed, but you usually set that aside when you're with an important customer. Could you imagine *not* smiling when greeting a customer? Snapping at him when he asks you to do something? Of course not! You could have the worst headache and ten things that have gone wrong that day, but when a customer calls, you put your happy face on and ignore whatever problems you're having. Is that so hard to do with your best friend? Try being Mr. Nice Guy at home for one week and see how it affects your relationships. (I'm not talking about being fake or anything phony; just the same basic consideration that you extend to any other customer.)

Treating them as if they are more important to you than you are to them. This usually means listening to your wife, paying attention to what she has to say rather than making her always listen to how your day went. If you are a single-income family and your wife is working full-time raising the children, this strategy is even more important because the "breadwinner" tends to act as if his work is more important. It isn't.

Using customers' names when you talk to them. The next time you

Is the Customer Always Right?

S. Gordon Selfridge, founder of Selfridge department stores in the UK, is credited with coining the phrase "The customer is always right." It became the foundation of his company's legendary record of great customer service. He believed that even if the customer is wrong, it is better to find common ground than to win an argument. Good advice for marriage. Psychologist and bestselling author Wayne Dyer cautions against the "attachment to being right," arguing that it creates suffering in relationships. "When you have a choice to be right or to be kind, choose kind and watch your suffering disappear."

watch a politician or business leader interviewed on television, notice how the subject always refers to the interviewer by name. It's done intentionally because it disarms the interviewer, turning a potentially adversarial interview into a conversation. It's also just plain classy. This seems like such a small thing, but it's really huge and says to your loved ones, "I'm fully engaged with you right now. You matter to me."

Listening carefully to your customers when they talk to you and looking them in the eyes so they know you care about what they are saying. No one likes to talk to a newspaper or someone looking down into his Blackberry, but so many times we practice our multitasking skills when talking to our wives or children. Would you do that in a conversation with one of your clients or colleagues? The simple act of setting the newspaper down, putting your phone away, and looking into your wife's eyes creates the kind of connection that nurtures the love and appreciation you have for each other. I guarantee you will also see things in those eyes that remind you, again, why you fell in love with her. It's difficult to be angry with or distant from someone if you're looking them right in the eyes.

Following through with what you say you will do. Sometimes we think great customer service at home means long-stemmed roses and candlelight dinners. Those are nice, but I'll bet your wife would forego such extravagant expressions of kindness if you would just do what you say you are going to do. Failure to follow through says, "You aren't all that important to me."

Showing empathy and understanding their needs rather than assuming you know their needs. I may regret this generalization, but guys tend to jump in and try to fix things before they really know what's wrong. Especially in relationships. It goes something like this: "Hmm. She's not herself today. Probably sad. Guess I'll cheer her up." Good intentions, but how did he know she was sad? Maybe she was in a reflective mood. Maybe she was worried about something. Instead of trying to cheer her up, he might have simply shown her that he cares:

"You doing okay?" Besides, often the best fix for someone is not to get fixed but to be understood and accepted. What do you *really* think your wife wants from you when she's sad: a dumb joke or a pair of arms around her that say, "No matter what, I'm here for you"?

Receiving their complaints without defensiveness and quickly addressing them. When a customer complains, they don't want to hear your excuses; they just want you to hear them and do something about the problem they are bringing to your attention. So why do we feel the

---

Not Asking for Much

Sheri and Bob Stritof have been married for forty-four years. Early in their marriage, they were divorced for two years, and then they remarried. They now present workshops on marriage, are the marriage "go to" resource for About.com, and have written *The Everything Great Marriage Book*. From their thirty years of working with married couples, here's what they say a wife expects from her husband:[*]

- Tell her daily that you love her.
- Understand and forgive her when she makes mistakes.
- Converse with her about things other than the kids, your job, and the weather.
- Say yes more than no.
- Listen well.
- Give her affection and kindness.

---

[*] Sheri Stritof and Bob Stritof, "Top Ten Things Wives Want from Their Husbands: What Women Want from Marriage," About.com, *http://marriage.about.com/od/marriagetoolbox/tp/wiveswant.htm*.

need to defend ourselves when our partners complain about the way we leave our clothes lying around the bedroom? She doesn't really care that you were in a hurry or that your mother never made you pick up after yourself. She just wants you to hang up your clothes! Treat her exactly as you would treat your best customer who called to complain about the job you just did for him. Find out what's wrong and fix it.

Turning off the cell phone when meeting with a customer. Cell phones are great, but they can also be intrusive. When you get home from work, turn it off, or at least discipline yourself to let incoming calls go to your voice mail so that you can respond later. Nothing says "you aren't very important" more than taking a call when you're talking with your wife or kids.

Looking for ways to compliment the customer. This may be the easiest and most effective customer-service strategy you can use at home. Easy, because there are so many opportunities to compliment your wife if you will just take some time each day to notice. Effective, because even the smallest compliment turns an ordinary day into a special one. Think of how great you feel when you get a compliment from someone at work. It puts a bounce in your step and motivates you to do an even better job at whatever it was that earned you the compliment. All from a few heartfelt words of praise. Why *wouldn't* you want to do that for your wife and family?

Going the extra mile whenever possible. I love trying to wow my customers, to go above and beyond what's expected of me in order to give them a great experience with my company. You can't do this all the time, but when you do, it's great to see the reaction. Do that at home, and it earns huge dividends. I remember once when I was in an all-day meeting, one of those exhausting ones that drains you by the hour. Finally, the meeting ended, and I headed out to the parking lot and, as I usually do, dialed Charita on my cell phone to tell her I was on my way home. I asked her if she needed me to pick up anything for supper. "No," she said, "but there is something you could do for me." She asked if I would mind driving quite a bit out of my way to pick up an appliance she had ordered. But knowing that I had had a rough day she added, "But we can do it some other time if you're too tired." To be absolutely truthful, I was not only too tired; I just didn't want to do it. And I knew Charita would be more than understanding, but for some reason I felt the need to honor her. "Of course I'll do it," I said, and about an hour later I got to see the joy in her eyes as I arrived with the appliance.

The Mondrian Experience

Some of the best customer service I've ever experienced came from the doormen at the Mondrian Hotel in Los Angeles. These guys are just plain awesome. After my first visit, they always knew my name and greeted me with the cheeriest smile and a "Welcome back, Mr. Upkins." If I had to be at a recording session until three in the morning and the hotel kitchen was closed, all I had to do was tell one of the doormen I was hungry. "What kind of food would you like, Mr. Upkins?" And then they would drive their own car to an all-night deli or restaurant and deliver the late-night snack to my room. If I was running late and didn't have time to drop off the rental car and still make my flight, they would call a taxi and take care of the rental car for me.

Of course, they were trained to do this so that I would remain a loyal customer. And it worked. There are a lot of hotels in Los Angeles, but whenever I'm there, I always go back to the Mondrian. They have earned my loyalty just by showing me I'm important to them.

That's what we do when we give our wives and loved ones world-class customer service. I'm convinced that your marriage can survive anything if you have consistently practiced at home what you practice at work with your customers, clients, and colleagues. And the beauty of it is that you don't have to learn anything new.

What a great way to win out over the competition!

9

Protecting
Market Share

THIS WASN'T AN EASY CHAPTER TO WRITE, AND PROBABLY IT WILL be a difficult one for you to read. When it comes to marriage, no guy likes to think about competition. About someone else making eyes at his wife. Or worse, about her enjoying that kind of attention. But it would be naive to think that just because you've been married for fifteen years and have children and get along reasonably well that you don't have any competition. You do, just like you face competition from colleagues at work and from other businesses. It's one of those immutable facts of life: if you have something valuable, there will always be someone else who wants it.

It's no secret that regardless of what business you're in, someone is trying to figure out who your customers are and how they can steal them from you. Just ask the people at Chrysler, Ford, and General Motors. In 1945, the United States gave permission to the Toyota Motor Corporation to start up peacetime production of vehicles. Toyota opened an office in Hollywood in 1957 and sold its first imported car in the United States in 1958. At first, these little Japanese cars were something of a joke in the auto industry. (The first model sold in the U.S. was called a Toyopet.) But the company paid close attention to the Big Three, and especially to what consumers wanted. So now, barely fifty years after selling the first Toyopet, Toyota has surpassed General Motors to claim the number one spot in market share!

Just a few years ago, GM thought it was too big and too successful to worry about competition from a little foreign company. Today, they are watching Toyota's taillights, trying to figure out how to get back in front of them.

Who's Your Competition?

Competition in marriage is more subtle and complex than the head-to-head battles we fight in business, yet it's no less a threat. In terms of market share, you started out in your marriage clearly in the number one spot. You earned that coveted position by beating out the competition—all those other guys and former boyfriends who silently cursed their luck when they saw that diamond on her finger. You probably didn't know it, but you used the same strategies to win your market share that businesses use:

- *Research the customer database.* Wow! There sure are a lot of cute girls on campus.

- *Determine customer profitability.* I wonder which one would be just right for me.

- *Develop customer acquisition strategy.* What do I have to do to win her over?

- *Establish initial contact with the potential customer.* Um, are you doing anything Friday night?

- *Showcase your company's benefits.* Wash the car. Find a clean shirt. Wear cologne. Show up early. Bring flowers. Don't make a fool of yourself.

Okay, maybe I'm stretching it, but you get the idea. You saw someone who was so attractive inside and out that you wanted to win her over, and you set out on a mission to convince her you were the man of her dreams. That's the head-to-head competition that's so similar to the business world, but once you said your vows, another type of competition entered the marital marketplace. For both of you. It's the kind of competition that can be as devastating as having another man steal your wife from you, and that's competition from anything that can overshadow you as the most important thing in her life.

For example, most marriage counselors agree that if a marriage is not strong, everything from children to work to hobbies can fill the void a woman feels when her husband does not give her the attention she deserves. In other words, if you do not protect your market share, your wife, by default, will invest more of her time and interests in other things.

That's what happened to Tim C., a great guy with a wonderful wife and three super kids. Tim was one of those guys who poured himself into everything he did. He was the CEO of a small credit union in his city. He was active in his church and Knights of Columbus. He was president of the athletic boosters at his kids' high school. In his "spare" time he served on the local United Way board. His wife, Suzanne, used her training as a social worker to mentor troubled teens at a juvenile detention center and thanks to a flexible work schedule was able to cart her kids back and forth between school, church, and athletic activities. A busy family, they always tried to have at least one evening meal together, which they used to get caught up with each other. They also protected two weeks annually for spectacular family vacations.

After their youngest child went off to college, Tim and Suzanne began experiencing problems in their relationship, something that was new to them. In twenty years of marriage, they couldn't ever remember having a serious argument. But now they seemed to fight about the smallest of things. Unsettled by this and wise enough to seek help, they began seeing a marriage counselor, who, after hearing their stories, concluded that despite being married for so long and without any apparent problems, they had let all of their good activities take priority in their lives.

Market Share and Marriage

To use business terminology, you are the number one vendor to your wife and children. They look to you to provide a great product at a fair price and to keep them coming back with great service.

Product. The product you provide is yourself—your time, your attention, your love. More than anything, your family wants you present in their lives. If you are absent too much of the time, they will look for other things to take your place.

Price. You're a real bargain. Or at least you should be. You offer yourself to your family for free. No charge. You place no conditions on your love. If they know that—really believe it—they will realize that they can't find a bargain like that anywhere else.

Service. Not only is your product free, but when it breaks, you fix it immediately. That means when you make a mistake, you own up to it right away and correct it. You don't hold grudges and you're forgiving when these most precious customers get upset with you.

When you provide your great product at such a bargain price and service it well, you get great customer loyalty!

"He basically told me that I had devoted so much of myself to my work and volunteer work that my wife, rather than complain or call it to my attention, transferred her loyalties to our kids and her own work," Tim explained. "She didn't love them more than me, but since they were more accessible than I was, they sort of took my place. Once the kids were gone, we both had more time to spend with each other, but instead of growing closer, we got on each other's nerves because we had left our relationship on autopilot for so long."

Tim and Suzanne's story could be repeated by thousands of other hardworking and family-oriented couples. Writing in *Focus on the Family* magazine, Teresa Turner Vining says, "When couples start out together, their marriage is usually their primary focus, but then kids, jobs and household chores begin to compete for their attention. All these distractions pull them from the helm of their marriage, and they drift away from each other. The drift can be so subtle that by the time the couple realize what's happening, they are already miles apart."[5] The late Louis McBurney, one of the pioneers in Christian counseling, says, "The sense of unity and fulfillment that is so essential to a successful marriage isn't destroyed by a single, cataclysmic event. It erodes gradually in small, barely discernible ways. It's only after a matter of months or years that we realize how far we have drifted apart."[6]

McBurney suggests there are seven common signs of the erosion of a marriage:

1. You find yourself looking for alternatives to being with your wife.

2. You feel increasingly irritated by your wife's behavior.

3. You depend less and less on each other.

4. You quit sharing important details and information about your life.

5. Your sexual interest wanes.

6. You begin to want to spend time with a member of the opposite sex other than your wife.

7. You withhold or hide financial resources.

Drifting apart produces feelings of loss and loneliness. Even if you remain committed to staying married, it will not be the kind of marriage that brings fulfillment and pleasure to either of you. But if your wife is feeling lonely and distant from you, she is vulnerable to the attractions of others.

Opening the Door to Your Competition

Ask any coach what it's like to be ranked number one in the season, and you'll probably get an answer something like this: "It's an honor, but it also puts a great big target on our backs. Everybody wants to knock off the number one team." To stay on top, great teams and coaches both know they can't waste any time patting themselves on the back but have to remain diligent and keep doing the things that got them there.

Competition can be a good thing. It keeps you on your edge and provides an incentive to excel. I welcome competition in my business because it always pushes me to do better, to give my customers every reason to stay with me instead of jumping ship to go with one of my competitors. Great businesses never take their eyes off their competition because they know how easy it is to become complacent. Whether it's business, sports, or marriage, taking your position of leadership for granted is a sure way to lose all that you have gained.

When Motorola launched the Razr cell phone in 2004, they saw their market share grow to 23 percent the following year, putting it at the top of the highly competitive mobile phone industry. By 2008, its share of the market had dropped to 9.5 percent. What happened? While its competitors Apple (iPhone) and LG forged ahead with the development of new, more attractive phones, Motorola rested on its laurels. By not continually seeking to improve their product line, they opened the door to their competition.

We do the same thing in our marriages when we take our number one position for granted. According to an MSNBC poll conducted in 2007, 18 percent of married women surveyed admitted to being unfaithful to their husbands, and the reason cited by an overwhelming majority of those woman was "the need for more emotional attention."[7] That ought to be a wake-up call for all of us. They were not looking for sex or money or even excitement. Nearly one in five wives have sought intimacy with other men because their husbands have failed to pay attention to them. What this also says is something we just don't like to think about: apparently there are men out there who are capable of paying enough attention to your wife that she notices it and eventually finds it appealing. How sad, when you stop to think about it. We work so hard in our jobs to be the best—to help our companies grow, to beat out our competitors—but fail to use those same strategies to protect our marriages from the worst kind of competition. In your business, if you lose a customer to the competition, it's just a customer, and you can always find others. But if your wife feels so neglected that she falls prey to the advances of another man, the damage to your marriage and to your family is permanent.

Don't Panic

I hope I've gotten your attention. In fact, I would like to think you're suddenly a little concerned about the competition. Sometimes imagining the worst-case scenario jolts us out of our complacency and into a renewed commitment to our marriages. I'm not suggesting that we're all married to "desperate housewives," but I *am* asking you to think a little bit about your competition. I'm married to a very beautiful and intelligent woman, and I would be a fool if I didn't realize that many other men would consider her a prize catch. I also believe that because we have attempted to build our marriage on a foundation of faith, the Enemy would like nothing more than to bring us down. I'm mindful of the fact that my marriage faces competition just as my business does, but what I've learned in business helps me deal with this fact without fixating on it or hitting the panic button. Here are three responses to competition that will prevent it from threatening your marriage.

Don't ignore competition. In a perfect world, there would be no competition. In our imperfect world, we pretend there isn't any. That's a huge mistake. Accept the fact, daily, that competition exists in your marriage. That doesn't mean your wife is interested, but it's a fact of life that you ignore at your peril. Knowing that you have competition will keep you focused on your wife and her needs.

Accept the challenge. When I hear that a competitor is trying to steal one of my customers, I don't get upset but instead I do a quick inventory to make sure we're doing everything we did to gain that customer in the first place. Are we still giving him world-class service? Are we following through on what we said we would do? If we've made mistakes, have we gone the extra mile to correct them? It's not about trying harder; it's about doing the things that you've always done. If you sense your wife is losing interest in you—that you are drifting apart—chances are you are not doing the things that won her over in the first place. Are you keeping your word? Do you still show her how important she is to you? Have you made good on the "guarantee" you made on your wedding day that you are hers and hers alone? Charita doesn't expect me to bring home roses whenever we feel ourselves drifting apart. (That might actually make her suspicious.) But she does expect me to get back to the basics of loving her as if my life depends on it—because it does!

Expect to win. We all know—and love—those teams that are not blessed with the best talent but still win. They just have that winning attitude. That same attitude is important when it comes to dealing with competition in your marriage. I'm not talking arrogance or overconfidence; I'm talking about a quiet belief that nothing that competes for your wife's attention can interfere with the love you have for each other. I'm talking about the knowledge that your wife wants you more than anything, and that as long as you give her your truest self, she will reward you with steadfast loyalty.

Your Biggest Competitor

At the end of the day, your biggest competitor is not your children, your wife's job, her girlfriends, or another man. Your biggest competitor is yourself. Many people are so self-serving that they can't serve others. We make ourselves number one, putting our needs ahead of everyone else's. No one really forces us to make our jobs so important that we often treat clients and colleagues better than we treat our families. If we grab the newspaper and hit the couch as soon as we get home, it's because we want to. We think we deserve it more than our wives and children deserve a few minutes to get caught up with their husbands or fathers.

Most of what we do to let distance grow between us and our families is by choice. If that's true — and I believe it is — then protecting our families from the invasion of outside forces also is a choice. We make decisions every day that help determine whether our families remain safe from the many things that compete for their attention. Planning a business trip during the week of your wife's birthday may not seem like that big of a deal, but I can tell you it certainly isn't a smart idea, so here's what I'd like you to do: Imagine being in your home and it is surrounded by a dozen men outside with weapons, all waiting to come in to hurt your family. You're getting ready to go to work, and when you look out the window, you see them there, prowling the perimeter of your property, waiting for you to leave. If you're late for work today, you may lose a big contract. If you *go* to work today, you *will* lose your family.

What are you going to do?

You may never have to worry about armed criminals outside your home. But make no mistake—if you don't pay attention, a more insidious enemy will find a way to get between you and your family. And these are customers you can't afford to lose.

10

When Your Customer Gets Upset

I'M NOT SURE IF THIS STORY IS TRUE, SO I WILL NOT REVEAL THE name of the company. But apparently a certain internet-service provider has a reputation for making it extremely difficult for its customers to cancel their service. Apparently, one enterprising customer tried to cancel his service, and after making more than a dozen phone calls over six days, he still was unable to get his service canceled. His anger gave way to creativity as he went into a chat room sponsored by this provider and typed in death threats. The company, adhering to its policy of not allowing such behavior in its chat rooms, canceled his service!

I'd like to tell you that I've never had a customer get upset with me, but I'd be lying if I did. Big time. I work with creative people—artists, musicians, actors, designers—and let me tell you. I can get five of them in a room and we'll have five different opinions about what we should do. Six, if you count mine. And I'm not just talking polite differences of opinion. Creative people wouldn't be where they are today if they did not hold out persistently for their beliefs. So yes, I've experienced my share of disagreements with my customers. And you know what? Some of the best results have come from those disagreements.

I don't care what the relationship is—business, family, friends, neighbors—you're going to have disagreements, even serious ones. How you conduct yourself during a disagreement will determine whether it hurts your relationship or strengthens it. In my opinion, we let far too many disagreements serve up negative results, both at work and at home.

The Myth of Harmony

A lot of couples make the mistake of thinking that harmony means you never disagree. That you're both on the same page all the time. But in reality, harmony is the unique blending of two *different* musical notes to produce a sound that is richer and more rewarding than a single note. Yes, there are times when it's nice to be on the same page with your wife. In music, we call that singing in unison, and it certainly has its place. But it's unrealistic—even a little boring—to expect that to happen all the time.

If I'm in a meeting and everyone agrees with me and each other, I start to worry. That's because I've come to see that forcing everyone to sing in unison often stifles great ideas and creates a false sense of unanimity. I mean, I'm all for getting along, but I don't think that means we never argue. If there's not a little discord in our relationships, it usually means someone's lying. To avoid conflict they just pretend everything's fine. While it's true that I like it when Charita agrees with me on a given issue, I would hate to think she's agreeing with me only to avoid conflict or, worse, just to placate me. If you and your wife never argue, I suggest you ask yourself what you're doing to make your wife feel as if she has to agree with you all the time. In my opinion, harmony means not that we always agree and never argue but that we've agreed to disagree so that we might reach a solution that could come only from honest and respectful give-and-take. The

Bible refers to this as "iron sharpening iron" (see Proverbs 27:17), describing what can happen when people disagree the *right* way.

The Wrong Way to Fight

There's nothing wrong with a good fight in marriage. You disagree over something. You both state your case and go back and forth and then somehow resolve it. That's what I mean by a good fight. But too many couples use tactics when they fight that make things worse and stand in the way of any kind of peaceful resolution. For example, consider the following examples of how some couples disagree with each other and then ask yourself, Would I ever do this at work?

Assuming improper motives. You're having a mild disagreement over whether to go to your parents' house over the holidays or your wife's parents'. Last year you went to your parents', and normally you would go to her parents' the following year, but your dad had a heart attack and you feel that a visit from the grandkids would cheer him up. But your wife counters that she'd *really* like to see her parents at Christmas. Then you respond, "You just don't really care that much about Dad's health." Hmm. Do you really know that? If not, why did you say it? Could it be that your wife just misses her parents? Don't assume improper motives.

Use of sarcasm. In the middle of an argument over whether to go to a basketball game (your preference) or the movies (her preference), you say something like, "Oh sure, you know I just *love* those girly movies you take me to." Sarcasm is a sure bet to heat up an argument. You're always better off just being honest and straightforward: "I know you aren't a big basketball fan, and you know I prefer action movies. So let's flip a coin, and whoever loses gets to pick next week's big adventure."

Talking over your opponent. Husband accuses wife of spending too much money. Wife tries to explain that Tommy needed a new upgrade to some software for a school project he was working on. But husband just keeps on talking, trying to silence her. Even if he wins the argument and she takes the software back, I'll bet *they* had a fun evening that night.

Name-calling. The argument escalates to the point where words like "idiot" or "stupid" start getting tossed around. Never a good idea. Some guys excuse it as being "in the heat of the battle," but name-calling is hurtful.

Yelling and screaming. By now, things have really heated up and the kids are hiding in their rooms. I understand strong emotions, but I also know that once you start raising your voices, it's time to go to your neutral corners. Children should never have to hear their parents yelling at each other. Arguing, fine, but never yelling.

Fightin' Words

There's nothing wrong with disagreeing with your wife. Just avoid these common errors:

- *All or none statements.* Avoid "You always" or "You never" statements. They are as untrue as they are inflammatory.

- *Bringing up the past.* "That's just like you. Remember the time you ... ?" Treat every disagreement as if it were the first time.

- *The in-law game.* Would you ever say this to one of your customers: "You're just like the guy you replaced"? Never say to your wife, "You're just like your mother." Or if you do, duck because someone's going to be throwing something at you!

Silent treatment. So one or the other of you decides to remain silent and say nothing, not as a conciliatory way to defuse the argument but as a vengeful way to punish the other person. There's another word for the silent treatment: pouting. It's childish and only postpones the argument.

Walking out and slamming the door. Walking out is the ultimate signal that the argument is over, but guess what? It isn't over at all. Nothing was resolved, which only means you'll probably argue about it again. And again. And again.

Marriage counselors tell us that we let our disagreements become overly contentious for two reasons: we insist on having a winner and a loser, and we let our emotions take control. These two factors create the perfect storm for, well, a perfect storm. Even the smallest

- *The gender card.* "Sounds like your hormones are acting up. Maybe we should discuss this when everything's back to normal." First, would you *ever* say that to a female colleague or customer? Second, then why would you even *think* that about your wife? Trust me, pulling out the gender card is like pouring gasoline on a fire.

- *The head of the house issue.* Some Christians believe the man is the "head of the house." Other Christians view marriage as more of a partnership. I'll let you and your wife decide what you believe about that, but here's some helpful advice: never try to win an argument by claiming that God has ordained you to be right. Pull out the "God card" too often and your wife might think it's time to revise her ideas about God. Do you really want to be responsible for that?

disagreement over something insignificant can turn into the marital equivalent of nuclear war:

"You're not serious about painting the family room red, are you?"

"Of course I am. I'm tired of it looking so bland."

"But red is too dark. It will seem so gloomy down there."

"Red is lively. A little wild and crazy. Come on, Mrs. Excitement, break out of your shell!"

This might seem like an exaggerated example, but anyone who has built a new house knows that arguments over decisions like which fixtures to buy, whether to put in carpet or hardwood floors, and yes, even what paint color to use are quite common. For some reason, we feel we have to have our own way on issues like these, and when we don't, we get upset. Many couples have divorced over building a house because they argued so much over practically everything. A friend of mine confessed that he and his wife argued for weeks over what color to repaint their house. "Looking back, it made no sense at all," he explained. "First, we were arguing over two slightly different shades of the same color. And to be truthful, I honestly didn't care *what* color we painted it, but something just sort of took over and I fought her tooth and nail before I finally came to my senses and apologized for being such an idiot about it."

Now contrast that with some of the disagreements you have with your customers or clients. I've been in meetings in which we were trying to make decisions about graphic designs. We typically have five or six different options and each of us makes a case for the one we think works the best for the project we're working on together. Like I said, creative people have strong opinions, and often we aren't shy about expressing them, nor are we timid when it comes to criticizing the other person's choice. But despite the rigorous give-and-take in meetings like that, we are always able to walk out as friends and more often than not go out and have fun together.

I think it's safe to say that not a lot of married couples go out and have a good time together right after one of their arguments. But wouldn't it be great if we could? Wouldn't it make our relationships stronger if we could have a good fight and then share a big bowl of ice cream together rather than glaring at each other for a few days?

So what can we take from our work experience to transform the way we disagree in our families? How can we have a good fight without letting it destroy our relationship?

The Right Way to Fight

In my business, and I'm sure in yours, we do a lot of brainstorming. We call it "blue skying," meaning the sky's the beginning—there are no limits when it comes to ideas. We take time before these sessions to remind everyone that there are no right or wrong answers, that each idea deserves a fair hearing, and that criticism of an idea is not criticism of the person who came up with it. In other words, we set the ground rules. It's almost like the referee meeting with the two boxers before the bell rings to explain the rules. Everyone knows and accepts the fact that we're going to fight, but being reminded of the rules allows us to shed the normal defensiveness that can turn a good fight into a bad one.

Over the years, I've made note of the various rules of engagement when it comes to disagreements at work. I've also done a lot of thinking as to how these might be applied to our disagreements at home. On more than one occasion, practicing at home what comes naturally to me at work has helped Charita and me have *good* fights that actually accomplish something and bring us closer together.

Agree to disagree. I know this is a bit of a trite phrase, but as much as we emphasize it at work, we never seem to consider it at home. It's as if there's something wrong with our relationship if we disagree. But if you and your wife or children begin each day with the acceptance that you will disagree and that it's okay, you will be more likely to disagree agreeably. It's really a mindset. Instead of beginning each day with the hope that you won't have an argument, start out knowing that you and your wife will probably disagree over something, *and that it's perfectly normal* for that to happen.

Think win–win instead of "I win." In our meetings, arriving at the best solution for the company is more important than any individual winning her point. Therefore, we look for win-win solutions. Your idea may not be absolutely right, but parts of it have merit. Mine may have a lot of good to offer, but some of it would be disastrous for the company. Usually the best solutions borrow from several ideas. In your disagreements at home, look for the good in your partner's suggestions rather than fixating on what you don't like. Try to reach an agreement in which you both win. (For more on this, see chapter 13.)

Ask more than tell. Steven Covey puts it this way: "Seek to understand before being understood." Don't just immediately jump on your wife's ideas, pointing out why they won't work. If they seem wrongheaded or ill-conceived, obviously you're missing something, because you didn't marry a person who is without common sense. Ask for clarification, for more explanation: "Honey, I'm just not getting it, but I know it makes sense to you. Could you explain it again for me?" We're often in such a hurry to sell our point that we don't really listen to the opposing view. Besides, asking questions is another way to disarm tension in an argument. It says, "He's really listening and is trying to understand my point of view."

Remember who you're fighting with. When we go into a meeting with a customer and we know it's going to be difficult, no one needs to tell us that there's a lot at stake. That doesn't mean we roll over and let the customer have her way just because we don't want to lose her business. But at the same time, we remind ourselves that this is a customer, one of the lifelines of our business. So we try to make sure our disagreement isn't disagreeable. That means treating her with respect no matter how heated the discussion gets. It would be a good idea if, when disagreements arise in your marriage, you remind yourself who you're fighting with. She's your wife, your lover, the mother of your children. Keeping that at the forefront of your mind will infuse even the most difficult argument with the restraint necessary to avoid saying or doing anything with a mean spirit.

Don't take it personally. One of the unstated rules of engagement in my company is this: if I attack your idea, I'm not attacking you. Buying into this allows us to have some of the most vigorous, honest, and productive disagreements. I need the people in my company to be like "iron sharpening iron," but it's the iron that needs to be hammered on the anvil, not the person holding it. If your wife wants to go south for a vacation and you want to go west, discuss the merits of both ideas, but try to separate the ideas from the individuals. Too many times in marriages, we take it personally when someone disagrees with us. When Charita rejects my suggestion that we go to the movies, I have to remind myself that she's not rejecting me. She may be tired or just not in the mood to go see a movie.

Think whiteboard. Most of my meetings involve a big whiteboard on which we can sketch out our opposing views, list their strengths and weaknesses, and usually arrive at a solution that neither I nor my customer had in mind. I've often thought it would be cool to have a whiteboard at home for the same purpose. I think the act of putting ideas up on the board releases them from our egos; we see them in their natural states, unattached to anyone. Trust me, I'm not really recommending that you go out and buy a whiteboard and pull it out every time you disagree. What I *am* suggesting is that in your disagreements you try to focus on the merits of each others' positions with the goal of resolving your disagreement rather than winning or losing.

Take a break. Sometimes we reach a point in our meetings where we aren't making any progress and are rehashing the old ideas. That's when we stop and take a creative break, get some fresh air, and let things cool down a bit. Breaks are great when it comes to fighting in marriage. Both you and your wife need to give each other permission in a disagreement to call a timeout: "Can we take a break and come back to this issue in ten minutes or so?" It's not a way to escape the issue or silence your partner; it's a much needed respite that often gives you a different perspective when you return to the problem you're trying to resolve.

Watch your language. I'm all for vigorous, even heated, debate when we disagree in our meetings, but I won't tolerate rude behavior. Put-downs, sarcasm, ridicule, and other forms of insulting language are childish ways to silence your opposition. Even if it works — meaning you get your way — your wife will surely harbor resentment. And if it doesn't silence her, it could incite her to match you in your rudeness. That's when the shouting starts and the anger leads you to say things you will later regret.

If all else fails, tell a joke. Nothing disarms the tension in a difficult meeting like laughter. Usually it's accidental — someone is earnestly trying to make a point and in the process spills his coffee in his lap and it just cracks everyone up in spite of themselves. Or there's always that one person who just has a knack for saying something funny at just the right time. A friend of mine says the best way for couples to fight is to "fight naked; you'll either die laughing or get intimate." Hmm. He may be on to something!

Leave the room as friends. I find it so amazing that I can be going at it tooth and nail in a meeting with one of my customers and yet we wind up leaving the meeting laughing and looking forward to the next one. Why is that so easy to do at work and so hard to do at home? Part of the answer, I think, has to do with the fact that at work we somehow come to a resolution, while at home we let things smolder. At work, we know that the meeting has to end at 4:00 p.m. so our customer can catch a plane, while at home there are no such deadlines. There's no sense of urgency to resolve the issue because, after all is said and done, our meetings are never over. Married couples have incredible stamina when it comes to keeping an argument going. I have no grand wisdom to offer here, but maybe we need to set a deadline for our fights, and maybe we just need to lighten up a little when we disagree with each other: "Okay baby, let's wrestle this to the ground, but can we agree that we have to resolve this one way or the other in one hour? And if we're still fighting after an hour, the 'penalty' is a trip to Applebee's for dessert." Then again, that might not work for me because I'd be tempted to keep the fight going just so we could have dessert together. But how can you fight over a double-fudge brownie smothered in whipped cream?

How I Avoided a Huge Fight

For the record, Charita and I have had our share of disagreements, and I haven't always been a stellar example of what I've written in this chapter. But sometimes I pay attention to my own advice. A recent challenge for us was what to get our kids for Christmas. Here we are, about to celebrate the birth of our Savior, and we're fighting over whether to get Caleb a basketball or a football!

But one recent Christmas, Charita thought it would be great if we bought Caleb a television for his room. He's really into video games and we allow him to play them on Saturdays. She thought it would be neat if he had a TV in his room, and one big enough to make all those graphics in his games come alive.

I disagreed.

We have two children and I thought it was a little extravagant to give Caleb his own TV. What does that say to Zoé? But instead of just trashing Charita's idea, I affirmed her by saying it was a great idea but maybe we should give the TV to both of our children. Had I done the usual "No way!" we'd probably still be fighting about it, but I listened to her reasons for getting the TV, affirmed them, and offered an alternative that she readily agreed with.

Then came the decision over what TV to buy, and here's where Charita and I are exact opposites. If we need a TV, I go to Best Buy or Circuit City and buy a TV. Charita, on the other hand, spends hours researching the various models. LCD or plasma? Sony or LG? Best Buy or local dealer? Now here's where it gets tense. After all her research, she settled on a TV that was considerably more expensive than the other models in that category. Personally, I thought the price was a little too high, but I suddenly realized that the best customer I've ever known had spent hours driving all over Nashville researching TVs and talking to salespeople and going online to determine the best overall value. I could dig my heels into the ground and insist she buy the cheaper model. We would probably fight about it for a while and eventually she would probably give in. Or I could decide this isn't the hill I want to die on. Charita is worth more to me than the two-hundred-dollar difference between her model and the one I wanted.

I made a tactical decision.

"Honey, you've worked so hard to figure this out. I trust your judgment. Get the TV that you think is the best bargain."

In about twenty-five years, I'm going to be an old man. Caleb and Zoé will be married and will have given me grandchildren. No matter where they live, they will drive all night if they have to in order to join Charita and me for Thanksgiving. As we bow our heads to pray before diving into the turkey and trimmings, I will look across the table and remember the night Charita presented her idea for buying a TV for Christmas and thank God that I had the wisdom not to try to win that fight.

11

Not Just Another Meeting

SOMETIMES I THINK WHAT I *REALLY* DO FOR A LIVING IS GO TO meetings. Wake up. Get dressed. Take the kids to school. Walk into a meeting. Then another one. Then drive downtown for a lunch meeting. Back in the office for yet another meeting. And finally end the day with a long meeting via teleconference. It's what I do, and I suspect you also spend a lot of time in meetings. Love them or hate them, it's how things get done in most businesses.

When the idea for this book was just a kernel in my mind, I began to list all the ways I work with customers to see if I could extract something from each of those interactions that could be applied to marriage. Things like customer service and strategic planning and communications were no-brainers. The skills we develop in those areas transfer easily to marriage and improving our relationships at home. Then I realized that since I spend most of my time with customers in various types of meetings, there must be something I could learn from the way we conduct our meetings. If repetition turns you into an expert, then I'm the world's greatest expert on going to meetings. Will that expertise help me in my marriage?

Why So Many Meetings?

Here's the dilemma most of us face: we all know there are way too many meetings, but we also know we wouldn't survive without these meetings. Meetings reflect the democratic nature of the business world. Decision-makers desire input even if they have sole authority to make decisions. And employees appreciate being heard, having the opportunity to influence decisions that affect the companies they work for. It is the rare leader who will ignore the input he receives in a meeting with his or her subordinates.

When it comes to customers, we need face-to-face meetings to strengthen and maintain our relationships. Sure, we communicate a lot with email and cell phones, but there's nothing like sitting down with your customers and doing business in person. People often share a lot of important information with their body language and demeanor that you never see in an email.

So as much as I sometimes dread going to yet another meeting, I know that regular, well-run meetings with colleagues, clients, and customers are important to the success of my business. But meetings and marriage? You've got to be kidding.

Honey, I'd Like to Call a Meeting

Okay, I'll admit it may seem like a bit of a stretch to have business meetings with your wife. If I turned one of the rooms in our home into a conference room complete with one of those fancy speakerphones and a whiteboard, Charita would have me committed to an insane asylum. On the other hand, think for a minute about all those reasons you go to meetings at work. You may not need to schedule formal business meetings with your wife—in fact, don't—but you certainly need the benefits those meetings provide.

For example, regardless of how you view authority in marriage,

I strongly recommend as much democracy as possible. In our home, there are some areas where Charita makes the decisions and other areas where I make the decisions. If she made some of those decisions without getting any input from me, I'd feel a little left out, just as she'd probably be a little hurt if I never consulted with her on *my* decisions for our family.

Likewise, I know I'm not an expert in a lot of areas where I need to either make a decision or take care of something. For example, I'm not really up to speed on matters of health and nutrition, but my wife is a competitive triathlete and pretty much a nutrition nut. So I need her expertise when it comes to making decisions about my health. I may not always like what I hear, but I know enough to pay

We Schedule What We Value

Have you ever run into an old acquaintance and after a quick exchange added something like, "Hey, let's get together for lunch someday"? But somehow you never met for lunch. That's because despite the politeness of your offer, you really weren't all that interested in meeting for lunch. And neither was he. If you were, you both would have gotten out your planners and punched in a date.

We do the same thing at home. Good intentions are seldom enough for us to follow through with what we know we ought to do. So make sure you take the time to put these family business meetings on your calendars. It's as important as those tedious budget meetings at work, and even if you have to cover some difficult issues on the home front, you at least get to hug the "members present" when you're finished and you won't get in trouble with HR!

attention because she knows so much more about this area than I do. So getting together if only to make some of those joint decisions makes sense.

On the surface, I know it seems almost too businesslike to schedule a meeting with your wife. I mean, it's not like we never see each other or even never spend significant amounts of time together. You would think that because we live under the same roof and share a bed that we don't really need any help maintaining our relationship. Or that living together and hanging out together insures that she knows how much I appreciate her. If I took that approach with my customers, however, and assumed just because we have a close business relationship it's always going to stay that way, I'd be in trouble. It's natural to neglect some of the basics about relationships. In fact, most marriages get put on autopilot as a way to cope with the demands of work and family, especially when kids come into the picture. If you don't address the ordinary decisions and responsibilities that come with marriage and family life, the resulting confusion will fester and open the door to discord. Great reason to have "meetings."

Just to be clear, when I think of meetings and marriage, I'm referring to setting aside special times specifically to make decisions and touch base with each other. Your meeting could be in the breakfast nook of your home or at a local coffee shop or at a resort for the marriage equivalent of a business retreat. I'm not talking about the dozens of interactions you might have during the day, or even a quiet time you might have together every night. Nor am I talking about a date, when the purpose is mostly just to have a good time together (and you need plenty of those). Instead, I'm suggesting that our marriages would benefit from carving out regular times to meet just to make sure we're on the same page with the myriad tasks and activities that are a part of any marriage. And here is where your experience with meetings at work can help you make these meetings successful.

How to Have a Great Meeting

First, a word of caution. Ease into this with your wife. Don't suddenly announce that every Monday at 7:30 p.m. you're going to have a meeting. Instead, share this idea with your wife first, and when you do, emphasize the benefits: "Honey, we've been so busy lately that I miss being able to sit down and clear my head with you. Until things slow down a bit, what would you say if we tried to schedule at least a half hour each week just to stay caught up?" (Just be ready to catch her—she may faint from disbelief!) This idea of a regular meeting shouldn't be presented as overly weighty or problem-centered; present it as more of a safety net to make sure nothing gets lost in the hustle and bustle of everyday life. And you may need to try this for a while to see what works best for you: "Let's try it for a few weeks and see if it helps or is a big waste of time." Then experiment. Meet at a coffee shop. Or combine your meeting with a walk through the neighborhood. Find what feels comfortable for both of you.

You might also have a little fun with the first meeting by sending her a formal invitation or giving it a corporate name:

To: Charita Upkins
From: Louis Upkins
Date: June 28, 2009
Re: Upkins Family Task Force for Better Family Management

She'll get the idea. (If I actually sent that to Charita she would probably respond, "Louis, have you lost your *mind*?" And then bust out laughing. Perfect.) I'm a big believer in the value of humor in marriage and this is one of those opportunities to keep things light and sassy: "Besides, baby, once you're on my Blackberry you're *sooo* much more important to me!" My point is that if you come at this all serious and businesslike, it will backfire. If you don't scare her completely out of trying it, you will at least have her so suspicious about the real reason you want to meet that it will be more of a barrier than a benefit.

Once you've convinced your wife you're not trying to go corporate with your marriage but just want to be more deliberate about touching base with her to make sure important details in your family life don't fall through the cracks, draw from your endless hours in meetings to make this an event worth repeating. Here are just a few of the things I try to do in my business meetings and when I meet with Charita.

Reserve the meeting space. At the office, that means making sure a conference room is available or reserving a table in a quiet corner of a restaurant. At home, it's deciding where and when you can sit down together without distractions. Meeting "offsite," if you can swing it, gives your meeting a special touch, especially if your wife is a stay-at-home mom.

Arrange for all your customer's needs. When I bring a customer into town for a meeting, I make sure a car is waiting at the airport to pick him up when he arrives. My assistant books him into a hotel designed to serve people who are traveling on business. If he's pressed for time, we will move our meeting to a location close to the airport so we can get our business done and get him to his flight on time. If he's never been to Nashville, I check to see if he'd like to visit any of our wonderful tourist sites, such as the Grand Ole Opry. I do everything I can to make this meeting a positive experience. Translating that to marriage simply means you focus on your wife's needs rather than your own. If Tuesday mornings at ten work best for her, change *your* schedule, if possible, to accommodate her. If she wants this meeting to be combined with a half-hour walk on the bike path by the river, get out your walking shoes. Use the skills you learned at work to give your wife the best experience possible.

Know why you're meeting. I recall a *Dilbert* cartoon in which several people are sitting around a conference table and the meeting organizer said something like, "There's no specific agenda for this meeting, so we'll just make unrelated emotional statements about things that bother us." Not a good idea in business and *really* not a good idea in your marriage. For your first meeting, you may want to take the lead in determining what the meeting is all about, but whenever you meet like this, both of you should be prepared and know what's on the agenda. (Not that you need a formal, written agenda, but you need to know what to cover when you meet.) Here are the kinds of things that would be fair game for your meetings.

- *Weekly schedule*—specifically special events such as soccer games, parent-teacher meetings, days when one of you has to work late, and so on.
- *Budget/money*—primarily unexpected expenses so you both know about them.
- *Decisions*—all the everyday "stuff" that needs an answer: "We're invited to the Johnsons' next Tuesday night." "Andy wants to have a sleepover." "Should we switch phone companies?"
- *Follow-up and updates*—"Were you able to find a hotel for our spring break trip?" "I finally got hold of my sister and they are planning to be here the day after Christmas."
- *Prayer*—not to overspiritualize, but I don't think husbands and wives can ever pray *too* much, so this is a great opportunity to pray together for each other and your family.

You get the idea. These are the types of things that often get ignored or forgotten until the last minute. Just as you would call a customer before the meeting to see what he wants to cover in the meeting, make sure you check with your wife ahead of time for the things *she* wants to address. None of this is earth-shaking stuff, but it can cause minor annoyances if left untended too long.

Make sure someone's taking notes. At work, we usually have a secretary in our meetings to record whatever business we cover. At home, you will at least want to have your calendars handy. But if you're like me and sometimes forget the things you talked about five minutes ago, have a pencil and paper handy to write down whatever you agreed to do.

Review action items. This is a great practice both at work and at home. It's amazing how often we just assume someone is going to follow up on a particular task or assignment and then it never gets done. That's why writing things down is helpful; you can review each other's to-do list and be clear about such easy-to-forget jobs as who's going to call the insurance company.

Confirm the next meeting. Just about every meeting with a customer ends with all of us getting out our planners and trying to set the date for our next meeting. If this type of regular "business meeting" is new for you and your wife, it may take a while to get into a rhythm, so make sure you both know when you're going to meet again.

It's Not All Business

Meeting organizers are always looking for ways to make meetings more tolerable and productive. I read about a manager who once or twice a year would throw out the agenda for a regularly scheduled meeting and turn it into a party, complete with party hats and noisemakers. It boosted attendance because no one wanted to miss the party and they never knew when he would pull it off. Some meeting planners always try to have food or drinks available. Others have upbeat music playing while employees assemble. I mention this because the temptation will be to make your meeting with your wife too formal and businesslike, and that will kill it. Sure, you have things you need to discuss, decisions to make. But remember who you're meeting with. Enjoy this time you have together just as much as you would enjoy a date. Compliment each other and celebrate when you cross off something on your list that had to be accomplished. Leave enough time to share the good things that are going on in your lives. Find excuses to laugh. If this meeting becomes too mechanical and feels more like an obligation—one more thing on your schedules—you'll miss the great benefits it can provide.

As recently as thirty years ago, this idea of setting aside some time regularly to connect would seem superfluous. The pace of life was slower and couples had plenty of opportunities to address the various things that needed to be addressed. Families then tended to have at least one meal together every day, giving them a built-in "meeting" to connect with each other. For a variety of reasons life has gotten busier to the point that family life sometimes feels chaotic. The traditional family dinner every night is practically as rare as a dinosaur sighting. Even though it may seem odd to call a meeting with your spouse, once you find the rhythm you will wonder how you survived without these family business meetings. If you have older children—middle- and high-schoolers—consider involving them. These will be your busiest years in your lives, with everyone going in a hundred different directions, but you will navigate this period much more easily if you take the time to make sure everyone knows what's going on.

If it still seems like a bit of a stretch to add yet another meeting to your life and to do it with your wife and family, consider canceling every meeting at work for one year. What do you think would happen? Is that already happening with your family? If those darn meetings keep your company running smoothly, maybe your marriage and family would run a lot more smoothly if you brought your meeting skills home.

12

Never
Give Up

NOBODY LIKES TO BE CALLED A QUITTER. IT'S JUST SOMETHING that's instilled in us early on. Ask anyone where the lines "I think I can, I think I can" come from and I'd be willing to bet they will cite *The Little Engine That Could,* still one of the most popular children's books of all time. In Sunday school we cheered little David as he dropped Goliath with one stone in front of an entire army of quitters. Our school teachers took extra care to point out that a great hero like Thomas Edison failed thousands of times before he finally created a working lightbulb. Winston Churchill failed the sixth grade. Abraham Lincoln lost his first election, went into business with a friend, and then the business failed. Albert Einstein did so poorly in school that a teacher actually told the genius, "You will never amount to anything."

A friend of mine recalled his first time at bat in his very first Little League game. Three pitches. Three swings. No contact. He was so upset at himself for striking out that he ran to the parking lot and got into his dad's car, determined to stay there until his dad took him home. As far as he was concerned, he was through with baseball. His dad calmly followed him, opened up his door, climbed in the driver's seat, and then asked him if he wanted to go home. My friend nodded and his dad started the car, but before easing it into gear, his dad turned and uttered these words: "Reggie Jackson [his favorite player at the time] struck out twice yesterday and then he hit a home run." In his second time at bat in his very first Little League game, my friend hit a home run.

As kids, we played pickup games of basketball and football at the park, and no matter how far behind we were, we never quit. Ever. We preferred the pain of getting massively thumped to the shame of hearing the other guys yell, "Quitters!"

This never-give-up attitude carries over into just about every other area of our lives, especially work. I've taken on some projects that turned out to be much bigger and more difficult than I thought they were. You know what I'm talking about—the kind that you promised to deliver in a month, and a few days into it you realized it would take three months, at least, to finish it. Calling your customer to back out just isn't an option; asking for more time is almost as bad as quitting. So you do what it takes. Eighteen-hour days. Seven days a week. And an all-nighter the day before it's due. You lose money because of all the overtime you had to pay, but you didn't quit!

Why is it, then, with all this emphasis on stubbornly refusing to quit, that we give up so easily when our marriages head into difficulty? Why are we so willing to pull all-nighters to please a customer yet walk away from our responsibilities at home, even to the point of ending a relationship when it hits a bump in the road?

Quitting Is an Attitude and It Becomes a Habit

When I talk about quitting, I'm not necessarily referring to divorce, though I'll get to that later. I'm talking about settling for a relationship that is far from what it could be because you quit doing the things that attracted her to you. I'm talking about accepting the distance that is inevitable if you don't work at things like communication, compatibility, and romance. Marriage is work—sometimes hard work—and some of us just don't want to exert ourselves too much when it comes to our marriages.

Early in our marriage, I struggled with a bit of the quitter attitude. If we had a disagreement over something—usually something pretty small—I would reach a point where I'd just walk out of the

When You Feel Like Quitting

Staying married isn't easy. Quitting is. If you find yourself secretly dreaming about being free from the cares and conflicts of your marriage, test your dream against reality by doing the following:

Conduct a personal "profit and loss" study. What will you gain from quitting? What will you lose? Will you gain enough to offset your losses?

Seek reliable counsel. Tell a close friend you can trust. Talking about it helps gain perspective. You wouldn't consider ending an important business relationship without wise counsel, would you?

Review your "corporate" history. Spend an evening reflecting on the earlier days of your marriage. Pull out family albums or watch videos of vacations. In times of conflict and stress we often forget about the better times.

Project future performance. What will life be like without this partnership? Imagine holidays, birthdays, graduations, and weddings as a "free man."

Decide on your knees. An old preacher once said he never made an important decision unless he was on his knees before the Lord. Good advice for when you feel like quitting.

room or leave the house if we couldn't resolve the difference quickly. It was probably learned behavior because I witnessed the same thing in my dad when I was growing up.

Whenever my mom and dad had a disagreement, he would just walk out the door. I'm not really blaming him because we all have to make decisions about how we live our lives, but almost from the beginning of our marriage, that's how I handled any disagreement. Just walked away from it. And from my perspective, it worked. It ended the argument. We didn't yell at each other or get into a big fight. But it didn't solve the problem at all. It just postponed it and actually drove a wedge between two people who loved each other very much.

We continued this pattern for some time, and if you had asked me about our relationship, I would have said it's great — we never argue. What I didn't realize is that it was only great for me. One day, as I was walking away from yet another disagreement, thinking I was being noble for preventing a big fight, Charita quietly but firmly asked me to stay. It caught me off guard because before, I was always able to make my escape and return a few hours later and everything would seem all right. Obviously, it wasn't, and I learned then just how wrong it is to handle conflict that way as Charita explained how much it hurt her when I walked away from her, how it made her feel unimportant and degraded, how it made her feel as if I didn't care about her or the situation.

Whoa! I realized that if I wanted to stay married I had to change my ways. As right as I thought I was, I was dead wrong. When I walked out on her, I was really giving up, a dangerous attitude that creeps into marriages like a stealth bomber. We convince ourselves it's the right thing to do, but it establishes a pattern that can lead you to believe that quitting is better than persevering through any problem you face as a couple.

I promised Charita that I would never walk away from her when we disagreed about something. And then I began to use some of the skills I use at work whenever a customer and I reach an impasse. I listened to her, even though I didn't agree with her. I avoided the temptation to interrupt her and let her say what she had to say. Then I repeated to her what I thought I heard, and listened some more when she told me I hadn't heard her correctly or misinterpreted what she said. Even if I still disagreed with her, I didn't raise my voice. Instead, just as I would do with a customer, I worked with her to find a solution that addressed both of our needs. And 90 percent of the time, we arrived at a solution.

Was it easier? Absolutely not. To be truthful, staying with her and trying to work things out was a lot harder than walking out of the room. And it usually took longer. A lot longer. Sometimes I had to listen to things I didn't want to hear. I had to pay attention and accept the fact that I can't always be right. But it was worth it because at the end of the day, my wife and my children are more important to me than anything else. Sometimes it takes going through some hard times to realize that. Quitting puts all the attention on yourself, while persevering helps you focus on what really matters in life. Every time I walked away from her, I was saying, "I'm the most important person to me." By hanging in there and working through our conflict, I was saying to both of us, "You're the most important person to me."

I'm convinced that if I had continued to handle our disagreements by walking away, I would have reached a point where our problems would have seemed too big to resolve and just walked out of our marriage altogether. Unfortunately, it happens all too often.

The "Easy" Divorce

I hesitate to say much about divorce in this book for a couple of reasons. For one, I'm a pretty positive, upbeat kind of guy, and any way you slice it, divorce is such a downer. Who really needs to be reminded how bad divorce is? I also had this idea that people who pick up a book like this are not thinking about divorce. You may sense a bit of drift in your marriage or just want to learn how to be a better husband, but divorce? Finally, I know that divorces happen to good people, and I don't want to sound judgmental.

But I decided to write about divorce because it occurred to me that with practically all my friends who have gotten divorces, it was a huge shock to me. Took me completely by surprise. All of these friends of ours seemed to have such good, strong marriages. One week we see them arm in arm at church, and the next week they're shopping for lawyers. Sadly, we can't assume that the smiling couple we occasionally have over for dinner isn't about to call it quits.

That's what happened with a good friend of mine, Roger, who owns a successful business. A few years ago he decided to ramp it up by forming several partnerships and expanding his market. His wife heard bits and pieces from him about his plans and, from what she was hearing, thought he was moving too fast. I met with Roger for lunch every week or so, and as this expansion was going on, he shared his frustration over his wife's lack of enthusiasm. I chalked it up to the stress that new business ventures can place on a marriage. Then one day at lunch he told me he had decided to move out of his home, get an apartment, and file for divorce!

Here's a guy who had been married for seventeen years, had three great kids, owned his own business, lived in a gorgeous home, and he was ready to move into an apartment. All, apparently, because his wife didn't like his business plan. I realize that most divorces can't be blamed on one single issue and that other factors may have contributed to Roger's decision to leave his wife. But I can't help but think that Roger—and thousands of Christian men like him—had been influenced by both a culture and a church community that seem to view divorce as inevitable and not that big of a deal. I'm certainly no Bible scholar, and I know that Christians aren't immune to the world's problems, but the Bible makes it pretty clear that divorce is a step that should be avoided at all costs. What I have learned over the years about God's "rules" or directives is that they are not imposed on us capriciously but are intended to protect us from serious harm. I believe God wants us to fight just as hard to save our marriages as we would our businesses because he knows how much damage comes with a broken marriage.

Here's what Roger can look forward to if he ultimately decides to divorce his wife. First, he's going to lose a lot of money. According to Mediate.com, a dispute resolution center, just the legal fees in the average divorce are between fifteen and thirty thousand dollars.

The Top Five Reasons for a Long Marriage

Sunrise Senior Living is one of the largest providers of senior living services, with more than four hundred and fifty communities worldwide. They shared the results of a recent survey conducted among couples who have been married fifty or more years. Here are the top five tactics cited for successful marriages.

1. Don't go to bed angry.

2. Say "I love you" often.

3. Always kiss each other good night.

4. Have a good argument once in a while.

5. Respect and trust each other.[*]

_____

[*] Susan Lewis, "Secrets to Long-Lasting Marriages Revealed in Senior Survey," Reuters, February 4, 2008.

In addition, because Roger and his wife have children, he will be required to pay child support until each child reaches the age of eighteen. The average annual amount of child support awarded in divorce cases is $4,300, so Roger would have to come up with at least another twelve thousand a year. And even though he lives in a state with "no fault" laws, because he was the sole income provider throughout their marriage, he will be required to pay his wife monthly alimony that will allow her to maintain her current standard of living—somewhere in the neighborhood of six thousand dollars a month.

But that's just the money—the easy part. The other costs are too great to assess any dollar amount. For example, he will lose some or all custody of his kids. He will not be able to tuck them into bed every night and say bedtime prayers with them. At Christmas and Easter and other holidays rich with family traditions, Roger may be alone in his apartment instead of watching his children open their gifts or seeing his daughter in her Easter bonnet. Every time he picks his kids up or drops them off, he will have to deal with his and their emotions. He may agonize over reports from a teacher that his daughter's grades have taken a steep nosedive or his son has been getting into fights. According to the American Academy of Child and Adolescent Psychiatry, "Young children may react to divorce by becoming more aggressive and uncooperative or by withdrawing. Older children may feel deep sadness and loss. Their schoolwork may suffer and behavior problems are common."[8] Despite the fact that divorce is common and carries less of a stigma for children than it did in previous generations, few children escape some type of harm from it. And sadly, the effects of divorce on children do not end when they become adults. Children whose parents divorce have a higher rate of divorce in their own marriages.

Roger is a hardworking entrepreneur, so I know he will weather the financial storm that will come with divorce. He's also a dedicated and caring father and will do his best to be present in his children's lives. It will be anything but easy, but he'll manage. But what I fear most for Roger is that he doesn't fully understand the biggest loss that his divorce will bring—the loss of a loving, intelligent, and supportive "business partner." I believe the most important business a man can have is his family, and when you lose your partner in this business, you lose your most valuable asset.

How Valuable Is Your Wife?

Believe it or not, economists have actually developed an intricate method for assessing the financial value of a wife. And certainly, whether or not she works outside the home, your wife contributes to your family's overall bottom line. But that's not the value I'm talking about. Earlier, I explained how we will do just about anything to keep our commitments with customers. In a healthy marriage, we have that same level of commitment to our spouses, and it has everything to do with value. For example, I love Charita, but I also value her. She adds a dimension to my life that makes me a better person. Without her, I would not be the person I am today, so in that regard, I cannot afford to lose her. Not because of the money. Like Roger and most other people as well, I can always make money. But I cannot make up for the loss of not having her in my life.

Roger thought he would be happier if he left his wife. Doesn't every guy who chooses that option? Unfortunately, however, it doesn't work out that way. According to a survey conducted by the Institute for American Values, divorce seldom delivers the happiness it promises. The survey found that unhappily married adults who got divorced were no happier five years after the divorce than were unhappily married adults who stayed married. Moreover, the majority of those who were unhappily married but stuck it out said that their marriages were happier after five years. So happiness for them came by hanging in there, working on their problems, and refusing to get a divorce. The data show that if a couple is unhappy, the chances of their being happily married in five years are 64 percent if they remain together but only 19 percent if they divorce. The survey asked those couples who stayed together how they turned things around, and endurance was one of their three principal answers.[9]

So at the end of the day, no matter how difficult things may seem in your marriage, never give up. Don't take what appears to be the easy way out of your current difficulties. If you do, you're probably not going to be any happier, and you'll lose what you have worked so hard to gain. I like the way the apostle Paul says it: "Let us not become weary in doing good" (Galatians 6:9). Refusing to quit when the going gets tough isn't easy, but it's the right thing to do.

Oh, by the way, my friend Roger isn't a quitter. He decided to stay. They haven't solved all of their problems yet, but they're facing them together.

You can too.

13

Nothing Risked, Nothing Gained

I'LL NEVER FORGET THE DAY I DECIDED TO STRIKE OUT ON MY OWN in the apparel design business. Up to that point, I had always worked for someone else. I knew what I had to do each day and that if I did a halfway decent job, I would get a paycheck every Friday. When the opportunity came to start my own company, it dawned on me that I would be giving up a lot of security. If things didn't work out, I'd be unemployed and possibly in a lot of debt. I would get paid only when I finished a job. And if a customer wasn't pleased with my work, I would lose her business. As I was trying to decide whether to go out on my own, I felt like I was at the edge of a deep crevasse. I wanted to jump across to the other side and I thought I *might* be able to make it. But I knew if I didn't, I'd fall into the depths below and maybe never make it back up. I felt like I had a fifty-fifty chance of succeeding. That was enough for me. Besides, at the time, I wasn't married, didn't have children, and was pretty young. Sure there were risks; there are always risks when you try something new. But for me, the bigger risk was what I would lose if I didn't give it a try.

Despite my nervousness and the real possibility that I could fail, I went ahead and jumped because I knew if I stayed with my current job, I would miss out on the potential for a better life—better pay, of course, but also greater opportunities to use my gifts and talents to their fullest. I knew there was a bigger world out there than the one I was in, but to get there I would have to take some risks.

I don't know of any successful business that hasn't had to take some pretty big risks. In order to remain successful in business, you must be willing to take risks all the time, to reinvent yourself to adapt to changes in the business climate, to roll the dice when your gut tells you to stay the course. In fact, it's the business that avoids risk that ultimately fails, because every opportunity for growth brings risk. You simply cannot expect to grow and thrive as a business if you don't risk. And most of the risks you take impact your customers. If I decide to go out on a limb in my business, it's usually to do a better job of serving my customers. When it comes to holding on to my key customers, business as usual is not the best policy. They are always looking for something better, something to take them to the next level, which pushes us to do things we might not have done if we were just interested in the status quo.

I remember the time I was approached by someone who worked with bestselling author and television preacher Bishop T. D. Jakes. It was at a time when Bishop Jakes was expanding his ministry, and this guy was given the responsibility of finding ways to make that happen. He came to me with a request to design and print a T-shirt that they could mass produce and use to spread the good word about Bishop Jakes. I knew immediately they would end up with a warehouse full of T-shirts, so instead I put together a comprehensive strategy that involved our creating a private label program and establishing a retail presence. The biggest risk for me was not coming up with a bigger plan but going with the original one and then always being known as the guy who helped T. D. Jakes fail.

I have to say that every time I've taken big risks like that—even when I've failed—I have learned great lessons in the process. Stepping out of your comfort zone is worth all the extra work and even neutralizes the disappointment if you don't quite get the job done. Not only is the additional challenge of the work itself invigorating, but seeing the look on your customer's face when you deliver is, to borrow from an advertising slogan, "priceless!" You can't live on the edge all the time, but you're really missing something if you just stick to doing what you've always done.

Settling for the Same Old Same Old

One of the biggest challenges in marriage is finding the balance between security and excitement. Most of us get married because we want the security that comes from having a spouse who is always there, a home to return to every day, and the traditions that mark our days and give us reason to celebrate our lives together. We gladly trade the excitement of the single life for the security of marriage. We use phrases like "settling down" when we talk about getting married, and we expect that we'll fall into comfortable routines and regular patterns of behavior. What we often forget in that settling-down process is that we are wired for both security *and* excitement. As we rightfully turn away from "sowing our wild oats," we fail to replace that adventurous side of us with anything else. When that happens we end up either allowing our marriages to become lifeless or we seek excitement on our own. Neither of these choices is healthy or even necessary.

Here's a little theory I have, one that would be difficult to prove or disprove: many people who appear to be happily married are really just coexisting. Just getting by. What do I mean by that? They are married but they aren't really connected. They live almost separate lives. They get along. They seldom argue. They've established routines that keep decisions and disagreements at arm's length. If you go out with them for an evening, they are fun to be with and appear to really enjoy each other's company. There is nothing wrong with these relationships. These are the people who stay married and provide stability to their families and communities. Coexisting is admirable because it means you have learned to be content with what you have. If we had more couples who were content with being just happy enough, the world would be a better place.

At the same time, these relationships give marriage a bad reputation. They suggest that being married is a step down on the fulfillment scale, that commitment to a lifelong relationship is somehow second best. It's what led that guy who saw a couple laughing over lunch at a cafe to conclude they couldn't be married to each other because they were having so much fun. It's a good thing to settle down, but that should never mean we settle for less. Less fun, less excitement, less adventure, less sex, less romance—the very epitome of a happy enough marriage. One of the reasons young people choose to live together rather than get married is that they have seen these passionless marriages and want what they think will be bet-

Risky Business

Need some ideas for taking risks in your marriage? The following are listed in order from easy to "I never thought I'd do that!"

1. Ask your wife to plan the next vacation.

2. Sign both of you up for salsa dance lessons.

3. Celebrate your next anniversary by serving dinner at a soup kitchen.

4. Learn a new language together.

5. Write a song and sing it to your wife for her next birthday party.

6. Take a weekend trip without packing a thing.

ter. (Interestingly, they eventually discover the "happy enough" syndrome sneaks into their relationships anyway.)

Taking Your Marriage from Good to Great

Marriages that are stuck on autopilot are good, but not great, and I believe God intended marriage to be great. Happy enough happens when we tip the scales in favor of security. Great will happen when we bring adventure back into the balance, and that can happen only if we're willing to take a few risks now and then. Because security is so comfortable, we have to be deliberate about preventing it from becoming the dominant force in our marriages, and that means getting out of our comfort zones. I can't prescribe exactly how to do that in your marriage, but I can share some principles that have been helpful to me, both in business and in marriage.

7. Train for and run a marathon together. (We did!)

8. Volunteer to go on a missions trip with your church.

9. Celebrate a birthday or an anniversary in a hot air balloon.

10. Sell your house in the suburbs and move into a loft downtown (or vice versa).

11. Take a sabbatical from work, buy a motorcycle, and ride the entire length of the historic Route 66.

12. Bungee jump—both of you!

13. Get your pilot's license—together.

14. Start a house church in your home.

15. Adopt a child.

Vary your routines. Routines can be helpful or they can become ruts. With your spouse, make a list of all the routines you experience together: Saturday night movie night. Breakfast together every weekday morning. He sleeps on the right side of the bed; she on the left. She always reads the Scripture passage during devotions. Christmas Day alternates between in-laws. Then review the list to see if either of you feel the routine has become a rut. If so, change it. Or just for the sake of adding some variety to your lives, change a couple of your routines to see what happens. Where is the law that says you have to do things the way you've always done them? Obeying that law can be a real excitement killer, at home and with your customers at work.

Plan for surprises. Most of my plans at work are made to avoid surprises. That's because customers usually don't want surprises. They want everything to go as planned. But from time to time, I like to plan a surprise, like springing an unexpected, off-the-wall design on a client when she was expecting something like the mock-up she approved earlier. (With, of course, her preferred design in my back pocket in case she absolutely hates the new look.) Doing business as usual will always yield usual results. It's the unusual that makes life interesting.

Make a fool of yourself. Think of all the things you do (or don't do) because you don't want to look foolish. High on the list for a lot of guys is karaoke. You go out to a karaoke bar on a Friday night and your wife tries to get you to pick out a song and go for it, but you stubbornly refuse with all sorts of excuses, including, "I'm a lousy singer." Of course you are! But she loved it that night when you were dating and you sang her favorite song to her ... out of tune. Or maybe you would never think of making a homemade birthday card for your wife because you aren't artistic enough. And yet it's often the foolish things we do that make the greatest impression and create a level of excitement that strengthens relationships. Back in the day, you probably wrote a few silly poems or pasted together a collage of photos for your sweetheart. So why did you stop? Here's a good rule: if you're tempted to try something that's really out of character but are afraid it might make you look silly, try it anyway and see what happens.

Think big. Successful pastor and author Rick Warren talks about "adding a zero" to your plans. Think you can sell 5,000 widgets? Then aim for 50,000. Stretching yourself exponentially like that will take you places you've never been before. Do that with a customer, and he'll be your customer for life. Our marriages become ordinary because we settle for the ordinary. Get out of the rut by doing something spectacular. If you normally invite a few friends over to watch the Super Bowl, tomorrow order tickets to the next Super Bowl, wherever it will be played, and reserve your hotel room. Regardless of your budget, you can always find a way to live large now and then, and the payoff to your relationship is worth it.

Live a dream. Gregg and Lorrie Granger dreamed of sailing around the world. They knew nothing about sailing, didn't own a boat, and weren't wealthy. But they sold their house, plundered their retirement account, took their three kids out of school, and did it. The plan was to do it in two years; it ended up taking four. Any regrets? Not according to Lorrie: "We wanted to leave a legacy for our children, but not a business or riches." If you find it refreshing that there are people like Gregg and Lorrie who will take risks like that, maybe you need to look at your own dream.

Encourage "what if" thinking. One of the best ways in business to innovate and thus take your customers to a new level is to ask, "What if we ...?" In other words, to be willing to explore options that seem outlandish or just out of reach. Yet at home we're often constricted by the rule book that says there's only one way to do things. Chances are, your wife fell for you because you were different. You marched to your own drumbeat. So what's so different about you now? "What if" thinking keeps you pushing the boundaries of happy enough so that you never have to settle for less than the best.

Never lead with a negative. Customers love working with can-do businesses, businesses that never lead with a negative. Even when a customer asks me to do something I'm pretty sure I can't do, I never begin by saying no. Why would you? Usually, if I think about it enough I can find a way to meet their request, and even if I can't, I might come up with a better alternative. But something happens to us when we get home. "Honey, I'm thinking about going back to school to get my master's. What do you think?" Tell the truth—if your wife asked you the same question, what would you say?

"Well, do you think we can afford it?"

"I don't know, sweetheart—it's been years since you were in a classroom."

Improving the "Happy Enough" Marriage

Too many couples settle for "happy enough." You can restore that newlywed spark in your marriage by getting out of the rut. Here are some ways to do that.

- *Have a little fun.* Think like a kid in love. Create fun moments that will bring some of the warm fuzzies back into your relationship.

- *Surprise her with your gifts.* Men are notorious for buying ordinary gifts for their wives. Skip the perfume or sweater and look for the unusual. Nothing says "I love you" quite like a kite and an afternoon at the park to fly it with her. Take a chance!

- *Break up the routines.* Think of your relationship as an adventure, not a habit. If your usual date is dining out and a movie, mix it up a little. Prepare a candlelight dinner at home, then take her to a concert. Or anything else except dinner and a movie. Get out of those ruts!

"That's a lot of work for anyone, let alone someone with a job like yours."

Those may all be legitimate concerns, but what's wrong with saying, "That's a great idea!" What's wrong is that it's risky, so take a walk on the wild side and be a little more supportive of your wife. Nothing like the adrenaline rush of rolling the dice and seeing what turns up!

Incidentally, this one hits pretty close to home for me, because that's exactly what Charita did. She asked me what I thought of her going back to school to get her master's degree. I could think of several reasons to discourage her from trying, but why? She loves to

- *Look for excuses to party.* If one of you gets a traffic ticket, celebrate it each year by taking the day off work and doing something crazy together. It takes the sting out of getting a ticket and gives you an excuse for having fun. Other annual party ideas: a pet's "birthday," the day you bought your first house, the day one of you discovered your first gray hair.

- *Try a new look.* If you're a conservative dresser, have at least one funky outfit and wear it on a date. Never grown a mustache? Grow one. Always had a mustache? Shave it. Changes like these are not permanent and contribute to a spirit of playfulness.

- *Touch each other.* There was a time when you couldn't keep your hands off her. I'm not suggesting outrageous public displays of affection, but it's amazing how reaching out to hold her hand can turn an ordinary moment into a special one. And if that leads to something special, enjoy it!

learn. She's smart. And we live near a great university. This time, I got it right. "Go for it, honey!"

It's All about Balance

It probably sounds like I love to take risks. But I need to be real honest here. I'm just as susceptible as the next guy to the gravitational pull of security and orderliness. I like the sameness that comes with marriage—someone to share my life with, the familiar surroundings of our home, and the routines we have fallen into. But I know how easily that can evolve into a false sense of security that leads us to take each other and our blessings for granted. I know how being loved and treated with respect becomes an entitlement rather than something that needs to be earned and reaffirmed regularly.

When it comes to my work, I'm one of those guys who is constantly trying to think outside the box. You might be too. But when it comes to our marriages, a lot of guys have to force themselves to get out of the box, because it really is comfortable in there. Comfort is good, but it can become deadly to marriage if it isn't balanced with appropriate doses of adventure or excitement. If you don't find ways to program the unexpected into your marriage, you or your spouse may look for it elsewhere. When I'm faced with a decision in my business that calls for me to take a risk, I always consider the risk in *not* taking the risk. More often than not, playing it too safe hurts rather than helps my business, and that can happen in our marriages too.

Or to put it another way, I've never heard a wife complain, "I wish my husband wasn't so exciting and fun!"

So go ahead and take a chance, just like you did when you were dating your wife. Maybe the biggest risk you need to take is to go back and become the guy she fell in love with in the first place.

14

Success Goes
Both Ways

A FRIEND OF MINE TOOK HIS LAPTOP COMPUTER TO BEST BUY'S Geek Squad to get it fixed. A music downloading program he had installed a few months prior had quit working, and after frustrating himself by trying to get it going again, he surrendered and handed it over to the pros. The techie behind the counter listened to my friend's description of the problem and then told him it would be a reasonably simple fix, estimating it would cost thirty dollars, their minimum fee for service work. The tech guy inserted a flash drive, clicked a few times, and performed other mysterious tasks before declaring he was done. But when they tried to play music, nothing happened. The technician apologized and now thought it was a little more serious, but believed he could fix it by the end of the day. My friend was in a hurry and didn't really need to listen to music on his computer that badly, so he handed over his credit card to pay for the work already done and said he would come back another day. He was quite surprised, he told me, with the technician's response: "You don't owe us anything. We charge you only when we actually help you."

My friend's story is a great example of what is often referred to as a win-win solution. Best Buy decided it wouldn't "win" its thirty dollars if the customer didn't "win" a properly functioning computer program. They would have been within their rights to explain, "Unfortunately, we still have to charge you because our employee spent time trying to fix your computer, and time is money." In fact, my friend fully expected and was willing to pay the thirty dollars. Why *wouldn't* a company take a customer's money in a situation like that? Because smart companies know that you don't grow your business at your customers' expense. The more you can help your customers succeed, the more likely you are going to enjoy a thriving business. As my friend said, "I'll be buying another laptop within the next year, and I'll be buying it at Best Buy. They gave up thirty dollars today, but they'll get close to fifteen hundred down the road."

Focusing on your customer's success rather than your own seems counterintuitive, but it always produces better results. In 1974, Burger King adopted the slogan "Have it *your* way!" to distinguish themselves from McDonald's. The jingle "Hold the pickles, hold the lettuce, special orders don't upset us" was a response to McDonald's policy of not letting customers decide what they want on their hamburgers. McDonald's felt it took too much time and therefore increased labor costs if they had to make one burger with only ketchup and mustard and another one with the works. So they chose their own success over the customers' needs. The Burger King campaign was a huge success and a great example of win-win thinking. It positioned McDonald's as this big inflexible giant that insisted on having its way, while Burger King was more interested in giving the consumer what she wanted. And by actually letting customers "have it their way," the company also benefited by increasing its market share. In other words, it discovered that it did not have to win at the customer's expense. Ironically, some analysts credit that campaign for convincing McDonald's and other fast-food chains to begin letting customers place special orders.

As a businessman, I need customers, and I need them to spend their money on my company's products and services. But I also know that if they don't get something in return that is of great value to them, I'll lose them. Or at the very least, I will have to deal with their complaining. So one of the first things we do when we begin working with a new customer is to determine how we can help them. Not how much we can charge them or how much money we can make off of them—how we can help them. Because we know if we can help them with something that's important to them, they will be satisfied and we will enjoy a great relationship. Of course we need to benefit from doing business with the customer, but when we both win, that customer will keep coming back, and that helps keep me in business. I love it when we finish a project and send off the invoice and the next time I see the customer she says something like, "Louis, are you sure you're charging us enough?"

That's when being in business is fun.

What Win-Win Looks Like at Home

If you've paid attention so far, you're probably way ahead of me and are thinking, "How can I apply this win-win concept with my wife and kids?" Good for you! The skills we use at work that are almost second nature really can be taken home and put to good use. That doesn't mean it will be easy to make your marriage stronger using these skills; it only means that you already have them and don't need to learn anything new.

Just as it would be disastrous for my business if I insisted on being right all of the time, our families suffer when we are inflexible and act as if we're the final word on everything. Win-win at work means growing your business by helping your customers succeed. It means resolving conflicts so that both you and your customer gain more than you lose. It doesn't mean letting your customer win at your expense; it means having a mutually positive experience.

At home, win-win means enabling your wife and children to be as successful as you are, being willing to sacrifice some of what's important to you in favor of what's important to them. And as you negotiate the daily conflicts that are normal in every family, it means trying to find solutions that address your family's needs rather than fighting only for what is important to you.

For example, my wife is training for a triathlon, one of those long-distance endurance races that include swimming, biking, and running. A person training for a 10K road race needs to train around forty to fifty minutes a day, five or six days a week. Training for a triathlon can easily require two or more hours a day, which is why so few people compete in triathlons; the time commitment wreaks havoc on family life. So obviously, finding the time to train is important to Charita, but with our busy schedules, it isn't easy. As we get our calendars out, it would be easy for me to point to all my meetings and business trips and just let her figure out how to get her training in on her own, but that would be focusing only on my needs. That would be the classic "I win, you lose" solution. Would I do that with a customer? Not if I want to stay in business. If a customer calls and wants to meet me in Atlanta next Thursday and I have something on my calendar for Thursday that I can't get out of, I wouldn't think of telling her there is no way we could meet. Instead, we would do our best to find a way to meet as soon as possible. The solution we arrive at may not be optimal, but the compromise is better than not meeting at all. More important, my customer would feel that her needs have been seriously considered and that I have done my best to meet them.

Charita's needs deserve that same kind of consideration, which means sometimes we have to compromise on our schedules and even go to extreme measures to make sure my busy schedule doesn't interfere with her training schedule. If I use the same win-win approach at home as I do at work, both of us will benefit. You've probably heard the phrase "If Mama's happy, everyone's happy." There's a lot of truth in that statement, but I also like to think it's possible and even more desirable for Mama *and* Daddy to be happy, and that happens when we think win-win.

What about Your Kids?

If you were raised with "old school" parenting, you probably knew it was "my way or the highway" when it came to any disagreement with your mom or dad. If Dad said you couldn't go to the movies with your friends, you knew not to plead your case because it wouldn't do any good. It might even make him mad enough to extend the ban for the next *three* Saturdays. Mind you, I'm not criticizing firm discipline and parental authority. When it comes to anything that affects the physical or spiritual safety of my kids, I'm pretty old school myself. If I tell them they are never to play with matches in the house, it really is my way or the highway. As I remind my children, this isn't a democracy.

But sometimes parents — especially dads — carry this attitude too far into areas where it isn't necessary, and that sets most kids up for resentment and rebellion. For example, let's say you have a rule that your kids have to complete their chores on Saturday before they can go out to play. Good rule. It teaches them to be responsible. It prepares them for the real world. And it keeps their bedrooms almost inhabitable. However, let's say your daughter wants to audition for a part in a community theater production, and her audition is scheduled for 9:00 a.m. When she asks if she can postpone her chores just this once, do you hold the line and tell her she has to get up a couple of hours earlier to get her chores done? You could, and I know some guys who might do that because they feel it's wrong to compromise — give in once, and they'll expect you to do it all the time. But what would you do if this were your customer? Would you take such a hard line? I doubt it. Instead, you would try to work out a solution that honors what's important to both you and your customer. Here are two or three options that, in my opinion, preserve your authority (a win for you) and enable your daughter to audition for the play (a win for her).

- Tell her she needs to start on her chores when she gets up on Saturday, and then finish them after the audition. Chores still carry the weight of being important, yet she still gets to audition.

- Tell her you'll help her with her chores so that they'll be done in time for her to audition. Chores still matter, but now *you* really matter, and she gets to audition.

- Help her negotiate a trade — her brother does both his chores and hers this Saturday in exchange for her doing both chores next Saturday. She learns yet another way to be responsible, she gets to audition, she sees you as an ally, and her brother gets to sleep in next Saturday!

If this seems like I'm making a big deal over nothing, it may be because you too have a little too much old school in you. It's a lot easier either to stick to your guns and insist she finish her chores or no audition, or to just cave in and let her skip her chores. If you wouldn't do either to a key client or colleague, why would you do it with your kids, especially over something as relatively innocuous as chores? Hold the line on stuff that matters, but for everything else, be an ally instead of a tyrant.

The Pause That Refreshes

I don't know about you, but whenever things happen at home that aren't exactly as I would like them to be, I want to fix it. Right now. Charita might start to tell me about a problem one of the kids is having with a friend, and I want to get right to the solution. And that usually ends in disaster. Probably the biggest cause of our unpleasant fights can be traced to my trying to fix problems on my own. Though I have good intentions, it's really a subtle form of win-lose, because I end up getting my way.

I have since learned that in those situations, Charita wants from me exactly what a client wants from me: to listen, get the full story, and then work with her toward a solution. How can we possibly arrive at a win-win solution if I'm operating only from my limited perspective? To be honest, jumping in like that is selfish. It assumes that I have all of the answers and invalidates Charita's needs and feelings as well as her potential contributions.

So now, whenever we need to solve a problem at home, I try to practice the same skills that have served me so well at work. I listen carefully and avoid the urge to interrupt. When she's done telling me about the problem and sharing some of her ideas, I repeat what I think she is saying. If I get it wrong, I listen as she explains it better so that I really know what is going on. I have found that when I do that, the solution almost presents itself. It's less of an argument and

Putting Win-Win to Work

Win-win solutions sound nice — everybody wins. But they don't just happen. When the temperature of a minor disagreement increases, walk through the following process together.

1. *Win-lose*. Here's the solution if I win.

2. *Lose-win*. Here's the solution if you win.

3. *Lose-lose*. Here's the solution if neither of us wins.

4. *Win-win*. Here's the solution if we both win.

Which solution do we really want?

more of a time of discovery, and that's because you always hear more when you are quiet than when you are speaking. When you give yourself enough time to digest the words and the heart behind the words that you are hearing, it creates the kind of connection with the other person that compels you to resolve the problem in a way that's best for both of you. Taking time to listen carefully gives me perspective and usually reassures me that between the two of us, we will be able to come up with just the right course of action. It also prevents us from raising our voices and engaging in destructive argument. There's something about that process that actually brings us closer through our disagreements. I think that is what the apostle James had in mind when he wrote, "Everyone should be quick to listen, slow to speak and slow to become angry" (James 1:19). It's almost a formula for harmony: if you listen first and then speak, you are less likely to become angry.

Right or Righteous?

In his book *Don't Sweat the Small Stuff ... and It's All Small Stuff*, author Richard Carlson writes, "Needing to be right—or needing someone else to be wrong—encourages others to become defensive and puts pressure on us to keep defending." For whatever reasons, we often feel that our main job at home is to be right. Or that if we are wrong about something, we will lose face with our wife and children. Yet it is that all-encompassing need to be right that often drives a wedge between us and the people we love so much.

The apostle James, after admonishing us to be quick to listen, in the very next verse puts "being right" in context for me: "for man's anger does not bring about the righteous life that God desires" (James 1:20). The need to be right almost always results in harsh words and hurt feelings. And at the end of the day, what does it gain for you? How does being right make you feel? Being right may be a small victory for you, but at whose expense?

Over the years, I've attended my share of funerals, and I've also had the pleasure of being present at banquets to honor great leaders and citizens. I don't recall ever hearing someone pay tribute to another by saying, "He was always right." No trophies were handed out because the honoree was never wrong. And although I'm not a Bible scholar, I do not recall any instruction from Scripture to be right. And yet, think of how many times you silenced your wife or children with your need to win, by insisting your way was the only way.

A friend of mine shared how her brother and his wife were always fighting. Apparently he called one evening to report that they were getting along much better. She asked him what contributed to their improved relationship, and he responded, "She finally has quit questioning my decisions." To which my friend replied to her brother, "How's *that* working for you?"

In other words, is having it *your* way really all that great?

Our calling as husbands and fathers is not to be right but to be righteous.

15

Deliver a Great Product

PERHAPS THE BEST WAY WE SERVE OUR CUSTOMERS, REGARDLESS of the business, is to give them a great product, to consistently deliver a product or service that exceeds the customer's expectations. Why is Starbucks the leading coffee-shop franchise in the world? Because it delivers a great product, while other coffee shops only sell coffee. Certainly Starbucks' coffee is great, but other coffee shops offer great coffee too. Starbucks' real product is the *experience* of drinking coffee — the ambience of great coffee, comfortable surroundings, cool music, fast and friendly service, wireless internet, and contemporary design. When given a choice, most Americans will choose a Starbucks over any of its competitors, even passing up those who offer cheaper coffee. Why? Because no one makes going to a coffee shop more pleasurable. Indeed, Starbucks' mission statement is "to develop enthusiastically satisfied customers all the time."

Starbucks knows what its product is and constantly works to improve it. What's so amazing about their success is that they have captured an amazing 40 percent market share but spend remarkably little on advertising. When was the last time you saw a Starbucks ad on television? Chances are, you haven't ever seen one, because until 2007, they had not aired a single TV ad. They don't have to, because their biggest advertisers are their customers. Their advertising philosophy is to deliver a remarkable product and let their customers do the rest.

I'm sure you're well aware of the product your company makes and sells, but what's your product at home? What is it that you consistently deliver to your wife and children that turns them into loyal customers? It's not your income or your job. It's not whatever status comes with your title. It's not the things you provide or your success.

The main product you offer them is you — the complete package.

So how do you stack up? If a sales rep had to sell you to your wife and children, would he be pleased with the product he's repping? If your family were surveyed by Customer Service regarding

How Are You Taking Care of Yourself?

What kind of product are you delivering to your customers? Take this quiz to find out.

T   F   I exercise thirty minutes a day at least four days a week.

T   F   I weigh no more than ten pounds more than I did when I got married.

T   F   I do not smoke.

T   F   I have had a complete physical within the past twelve months.

T   F   I regularly perform "manual labor" chores such as mowing the lawn, working in the garden, or raking leaves.

T   F   I have at least one close friend, other than my wife, with whom I meet regularly to share what's really going on in my life.

their satisfaction with the product, how would they rate you? Like Starbucks, are you constantly trying to improve the product your family receives? Do you deliver "enthusiastically satisfied customers all the time"?

Okay, we all have our bad days, and none of us is perfect, but you have to admit that when you think of yourself as your family's product, it puts things in a whole new perspective. In business, I have to deliver a great experience to every customer, every time we partner on a new project. I have to win their allegiance every time we work together. I have to give them the best product if I want our relationship to be dynamic and long lasting. If I want that same type of

T F   I enjoy a hobby or other relaxing activity at least once a week.

T F   I carve out time for myself.

T F   I have read (or listened to) at least two books during the past year.

T F   I worship regularly with my family in church.

Number of True Answers

10   You are a new and improved product. Congratulations!

8–9   Your customers are satisfied. Now turn them into raving fans.

5–7   Customer Service has been getting complaints.

0–4   Time for a redesign.

relationship at home, shouldn't I at least pay attention to the product I'm giving my family?

After the Sale

When I have an opportunity to sign up a new customer, I do my best to showcase my company. You might even call it showing off. I show them examples of our best work and explain why we are the best possible agency to get the job done for them. If we get the contract, we do our best to exceed the customer's expectations, and from that point on, we work as if we have to win them over again. We evaluate every project and find ways to do a better job the next time because it's usually easier to keep a customer than to go out and find a new one.

Contrast that with the "product development program" in your marriage. When you first met your wife, you implemented your best customer recruitment strategy. You bought her flowers. You took her to the best restaurants you could afford. You probably spent more than a little time in front of the mirror making sure your hair looked good and your clothes fit just right. Even if you drove an old beater, you cleaned out all the old fast-food wrappers and hosed off as much of the road grime as you could. You arrived on time, opened doors for her, and offered her your arm. And on the way to the movies, you did your best to impress her with your witty charm. You were pretty sure you were the best thing that could ever happen to her, but you wanted to make sure she felt that way too. It must have worked, because now you're married and have a couple of kids and things are going pretty well. Or at least that's what we like to think.

But what if we treated ourselves the way we treat the products and services we offer to our customers? What if you viewed every interaction with your wife as an opportunity to win her over again? When she said "I do," your wife signed on for the long haul based on what she observed during your courtship. You obviously presented a pretty attractive product. When I see signs of trouble in a relationship with one of my customers, one of the things we do is take a good hard look at the product we delivered. Did we give the customer the product we promised? What if we did the same thing in marriage? Better yet, instead of waiting until things go south, what if we developed our own product improvement plans so that we give the very best of ourselves every day to our families?

Fine-Tuning a Great Product

I realize that returning to our dating habits may seem a bit extreme or unrealistic. If I started bringing flowers home to Charita every night, she'd be more than a little upset, and probably suspicious as well. Upset that I'm spending so much money on flowers, and wondering what I did wrong to think I needed to buy her roses. There's a certain settling in as a couple that's healthy and expected. One of the wonderful things about marriage is that it *is* possible to be your truest self and still be loved. You learn that the first time you wake up together; if she still loves you with your morning breath, she must really love you.

But togetherness and familiarity are no excuse for letting yourself go either. So I'd like to suggest three areas where we will benefit from constantly evaluating and improving the product we give to our wives: ourselves.

Physical

If you have a family photo album, find a snapshot of yourself from the first or second year of your marriage. Recognize that guy? You probably look a lot better now than you did with your 1980s hairstyle, but in all seriousness, most of us show the effects of too many business dinners and too many hours sitting behind a desk. Guess what? Your wife still loves every inch of your expanded waistline. She just wants to make sure she has you around for as long as possible. A lot of guys make the mistake of thinking they need to lose weight to remain attractive to their wives, which leads to a lot of questionable diets or weight loss methods. When Charita suggested I find a way to start exercising, it wasn't because she thought I was fat. (I actually can still fit into the tuxedo I wore at our wedding and use that as a way to make sure I'm not gaining too much weight.) She wants me to adopt a healthy lifestyle and to help her model that kind of lifestyle for our kids. She knows that men in stressful careers often develop unhealthy lifestyles, and she also knows one of the biggest health problems for kids is childhood obesity.

One of the ironies of "the good life"—which is what most middle class Americans enjoy—is that it's actually harmful to your health. Our jobs require very little physical labor but often cause greater stress. We have wonderfully rich diets thanks to modern agriculture. And all the labor-saving options at home (if you don't own a self-propelled lawn mower, it's because you use a landscape service) contribute to our sedentary lifestyles. So to avoid the early onset of heart disease, hypertension, and other life shortening diseases, we have to program physical activity into our lives.

The good news is that you don't have to train for a marathon to reap the benefits of a healthier lifestyle. Twenty to thirty minutes a day of walking at a brisk pace will improve your heart's health and prevent additional weight gain. But there are other little things you can do that will add years to your life and life to your years.

- Moderate your diet to reduce bad things like fat and sugar and increase good things like fruits, vegetables, and whole grains.
- Eliminate late-night snacking, or choose healthier snacks.
- Avoid skipping meals; you actually end up overeating later.

- Drink six to eight glasses of water each day; it helps curb your appetite, plus it's good for you.

- If it's four floors or less, take the stairs.

- Get up from your desk once each hour and "manage by walking around."

- Park your car in the less desirable spots to add a little more walking to your day.

- Play with your kids in the back yard.

- DIY (do it yourself); washing your own car is a great way to improve flexibility, raking leaves improves upper body strength, and pushing a lawn mower is great aerobic exercise.

Not everyone can do everything on that list, but anyone can select two or three things that over time contribute to a healthier lifestyle. Obviously, you benefit from better health, but your family does too because you are giving them the best possible version of yourself.

Emotional and Psychological

Regardless of what type of work you do, I can guarantee it carries with it enormous stress. We're all expected to work harder and smarter, to accomplish more with less help, and to do it all under budget. If it doesn't drive you to drink, it at least makes you a less than pleasant person to be around. Few of us are the carefree, fun-loving guys our wives married, and I can almost hear you shouting, "Amen to that!"

We all have different ways of dealing with stress, but most of us have difficulty admitting that it's a problem for us or talking to our colleagues about it. Somehow, we feel as if it is a sign of weakness to admit that the stress of our work is a problem. In fact, we almost wear it as a badge of courage around our colleagues. ("Last week I put in fifty-two hours on the Reynolds account!") Unfortunately, toughing it out takes its toll at home. We're less patient, quicker to respond harshly, and just a lot less fun than the original model we sold to our wives. Whoever said "Stress kills" is right. Not only is it bad for your health, but it kills relationships as well.

The truth is, life *was* a lot more carefree when you were dating your wife and in the first years of your marriage. Yes, we all experience pressure when we begin our careers, but not the "weight of the world" kind of stress that comes as you're given more responsibilities. When I started out, if my business failed, it affected one person: me. Today, I have a payroll to meet. Every decision I make affects not only me but also whether my employees can make their mortgage payments and their children can stay in college. That's big-time stress, and if I don't pay attention, it can turn me into something even my wife doesn't recognize.

I'm no expert on stress management, but I've learned from others who are. Here are the kinds of things that keep the ill effects of stress at bay so that you can be the best you for your wife and kids.

Exercise. Not only is exercise good for your physical health, it is as good for the mind and soul as it is for the body. Avid exercisers say they work out more for the emotional health benefits than the physical ones.

Deep breathing. Here's something you can do almost anywhere. Several times a day, sit straight up and inhale deeply, then slowly exhale. Repeat five or six times. Deep breathing infuses the blood with extra oxygen and also stimulates the body to release tranquilizing endorphins. It is one of the simplest yet most effective stress-management techniques. You can do it anywhere, anytime, and it becomes even more effective with practice.

Set aside some quiet time. Try to find at least ten minutes during each day when you can be free from your phone or other interruptions—and your commute doesn't count, because that's usually stressful. Use the time to meditate or pray. Reflect on the good that's in your life. Listen to soothing music. Try not to think about work or other responsibilities, and try to do this the same time each day so that it becomes a healthy habit you look forward to.

Write in a journal. Sometimes working out your frustrations on paper gives you a new perspective on the things that are causing you stress. It also allows you to leave the stress in your journal rather than carry it with you.

Reduce caffeine and sugar. The effects of stress are magnified by being wired by these two common substances. Caffeine also interferes with your sleep, which can add to your stress.

Leave work at the office. I realize this is becoming harder to do, but nothing adds to your stress like knowing you have some more work to do before you go to bed. It's better to stay at the office and finish up your work than to get home on time but spend the evening hunched over your laptop or connected to your Blackberry.

Spend time in nature. Most of us live or work within five minutes of a park that our tax dollars pay for. Fresh air, green grass, trees, ducks swimming in a pond, sunshine — all contribute to a feeling of well-being and help reduce the effects of stress. If you have a choice between eating a sandwich at your desk and eating it on a park bench, choose the park bench as often as possible.

Invest in friendships. Do you have a "go to guy" you can hang out with? You should. According to the Mayo Foundation for Medical Education and Research, "More friends, less stress."[10]

Find something to play with. Find a hobby. Play a sport or a musical instrument. Have a regular fun activity that you look forward to. All work and no play not only makes you dull, it compounds your stress. Writing in the *Harvard Business Review*, business analyst Steve Jurvetson explains why he launches model rockets in his spare time: "Besides being flat-out fun, rocketry helps preserve my child-like mind."

Spiritual

To complete your "product review," I'll begin with this question, one that I regularly ask myself: are you the man of God your wife and children desire to see? This is not about headship or who is the leader in the home. I'm talking about paying attention to the spiritual disciplines that allow you to be the best husband and father possible. I know from my own experience and from observing other men in business that this is an area that is often the first to go when the going gets a little rough—which it will. But I also know that I will enjoy a stronger marriage if I maintain my spiritual health. According to a survey published in the *Journal for the Scientific Study of Religion* in 2003, "inner religious commitment coupled with church attendance was associated with a reduced tendency to engage in extramarital affairs."[11]

The truth is, most of us know the things we need to do to remain strong in our faith. We just get lazy. Or we let other things take priority. I see this especially as men become more successful at work. It's never a deliberate turning away from God; rather it's a gradual sliding away from the life of faith. If we continue to let our spiritual lives grow cold, it drastically affects the product that we offer our families. They expect and deserve the godly man we aspire to be deep in our hearts, but if we don't pay attention to this dimension of our lives, we will disappoint them.

Like I said, you probably know what you need to do to grow spiritually, but some of those things are worth mentioning. Few things do a better job of keeping a guy on track spiritually than meeting regularly with a couple of other guys to pray for and support each other in the faith. I also think it's important to pray with your wife each day. Your "professional development" curriculum should also include reading (or listening to on your commute) great books by Christian authors who can help us grow in our faith. (Rather than list specific books, I'd recommend just about anything written by

John Eldridge, Philip Yancey, John Ortberg, Max Lucado, Dallas Willard, Rob Bell, Donald Miller, or Charles Swindoll.)

They Deserve the Best

Isn't it funny how when it comes to material things, we want our families to have the very best? I work hard every day, and part of the reason I try to be successful is so that I can give Charita and the kids a nice home, a safe comfortable car, video games, and the like. Nothing wrong with that, as far as I'm concerned. Short of spoiling them, providing for your family is admirable. They deserve the best we can afford.

What I'm suggesting in this chapter is that we ought to have that same attitude about ourselves. If our kids deserve the best pair of shoes we can afford, how much more do they deserve the best dad we can give them? If our wives deserve the best home we can provide, how much more do they deserve—and want—the best husbands we can possibly be?

You know something else? *You* deserve your very best too!

16

Celebrate
Your Success

IT'S CRUNCH TIME. YOUR COMPANY BID ON A JOB THAT YOU KNEW was bigger than you could handle, but with the way things have gone lately, you can't afford passing up work. Any work. You promised ten thousand units to arrive on Monday, and you already missed the last freight pickup for the weekend. With a little luck and a lot of overtime, you might be able to rent a truck and deliver the product yourself. It's that important. You leave the plant late Saturday, hoping and praying that nothing breaks down overnight. Your foreman calls you at home late Sunday morning and gives you the news: the last box is on the pallet, ready to go. Owning a small business has its perks, but on Monday morning, you're a truck driver. Three hundred miles and eight hours later, you pull into your driveway in time to help your wife tuck the kids in bed. The next day, just before lunch, your secretary walks in carrying a large envelope. "A courier service just delivered this," she said. You open it and pull out a gift certificate to the best restaurant in town and a small handwritten note: "Great job!"

You know the feeling, right? Being recognized for a job well done is almost better than the money. When it happens to me, it makes me want to work harder and try to do an even better job the next time. I don't know anyone who doesn't like to be praised, which is why I look for ways to reward my customers and colleagues. One of the signs of a great organization is its willingness to celebrate its success, both with its employees and with its customers.

It's also the sign of a great marriage.

Let's face it, marriage is hard work. Writing in their book *Fit to Be Tied*, Bill and Lynne Hybels estimate that roughly 25 percent of all marriages are relatively free of conflict and misunderstanding while the rest are just plain hard work. (By the way, the founding pastor of Willow Creek Community Church and his wife freely admit they're in the 75 percent category, so we're in pretty good company.) Some couples just seem to handle all the potential annoyances in marriage with almost superhuman grace and appear to coast along in blissful harmony. The rest of us may also have good marriages, but it takes a lot of work and paying attention and cleaning up after those times we've turned it into a mess. I'm not complaining about the work; it's worth it. But in addition to working hard to build good marriages, we need to take the time and make the effort to celebrate them as well.

I'm guessing you don't always celebrate the small victories that occur so often in your marriage. Neither do I. But when I consider how great organizations look for ways to celebrate internally and with their customers, it just makes sense to take that practice into our homes. Properly celebrating our successes at work accomplishes three things that are as important in our marriages as they are in our careers: it rewards extraordinary performance, builds loyalty, and enriches your environment.

Reward Extraordinary Performance

It has been said that in business you get what you reward. If you want an increase in sales, reward those who exceed their sales quotas. If you want to cut expenses, give bonuses to the divisions that come in under budget. Once when my team was working on a particularly challenging project, I noticed that Jerry, one of my team members, was still at his desk when I left the office, and most mornings was there when I arrived. Everyone else on the team was certainly pulling their weight and doing a great job too, but Jerry was really going the extra mile. He even came in over a holiday to spend time on his part of the project. Everyone on my team is salaried, so all his extra work wouldn't make a difference in his paycheck. We finished the job right on time, and I have to admit, we blew our customer away. I had already decided that everyone on the team would get a bonus that year because they all worked extremely hard on this important project. But as soon as the project was finished, I pulled Jerry aside and told him his extra effort had earned him a significant raise and that as a little extra measure of my appreciation, he would be getting some time off along with some tickets to catch a bowl game in which one of his favorite teams was playing.

Leaders and managers in great organizations go out of their way to try to catch people in the act of doing something right. What would happen in your home if you adopted that attitude? What if you recognized the many times your wife or your children did the right thing instead of noticing only when they made a mistake or disappointed you? For some reason we find it easier to complain about or find fault with or correct the people we live with. Every day, your wife invests a bit of her soul into you. If she has chosen to stay at home, she most likely set a career aside so that she could nurture your children and give you the opportunity to be successful in your career. That alone deserves at least a grateful heart toward her every day, and at least the gift of a smile and a kind word. If she works outside of the home, she's not only contributing to the family's financial well-being, but she somehow does it and still manages her other jobs: wife and mom.

I know, your wife isn't your employee, but when you stop to think about her "performance," there isn't a person on earth who does for you what she does. And puts up with all your faults as well. I love the scene in the musical *Fiddler on the Roof* in which Tevye asks his wife of twenty-five years if she loves him. His wife, Golde, answers, "For twenty-five years I've washed your clothes / Cooked your meals, cleaned the house / Given you children, milked your cow / After twenty-five years, why talk about love right now?"

But that's not enough for Tevye. Alluding to the fact that the first time he met her was on their wedding day and that his father told him they would learn to love each other, he asks again: "Do you love me?"

"I'm your wife!"

"I know! But do you love me?"

"For twenty-five years I've lived with him / Fought with him, starved with him / Twenty-five years my bed is his / If that's not love, what is?"

In other words, the ordinariness of marriage is really quite extraordinary and deserves to be celebrated. Toward the end of this touching duet in the musical, they both agree that they have always loved each other, and harmonize with these concluding words: "It doesn't change a thing / But even so / After twenty-five years / It's nice to know."

It *is* nice to know, and it's nice to celebrate that steady, loyal devotion to you.

Build Loyalty

Anyone in business knows it's cheaper to keep a customer than to go out and find a new one. And to keep your good customer, you can't rely on business as usual. You need to make sure your customer knows how much you value them, and one of the best ways to do that is to celebrate your successes together. Whenever we finish a major project for one of our customers, we try to find some way to celebrate that event with them. It doesn't have to be elaborate or expensive, though we've enjoyed our share of elegant meals with our key customers. When we take the time to recognize our customers and celebrate our successes together, our customers reciprocate by giving us their loyalty.

Too many of us assume that loyalty in a marriage is a given, a guarantee. That's a big mistake. It's one thing to be confident that your wife loves you, is faithful to you, and wants to be married to you until death. But confidence should never open the door to complacency. Your wife's loyalty is not an entitlement but a gift. Marriages go stale when men forget that. But they thrive when we show appreciation for the loyalty we receive from our wives.

In one of his famous Lake Woebegon monologues, humorist Garrison Keillor shared a touching story about a couple who had been married for forty years. Every night, the wife set the same plate of veal cutlets in front of her husband. Every night over the course of four decades, the husband devoured the cutlets, wiped his face with a napkin, pushed his chair away from the table, and looked his wife in the eye. He smiled at her and spoke in a tender voice, "That's the best you've ever done."

Wow! The old guy could have complained from the beginning, "Veal cutlets *again*?" Or he could have just resigned himself to the fact that this was as good as it gets. Instead, he turned the ordinary into a reason to celebrate. I'm guessing the old Lutheran married after living by himself a few years and was so grateful that he didn't have to cook for himself anymore that he decided to turn every meal into a banquet and honor his wife for preparing it. In his offbeat way, I think Keillor was making a statement about marriage: if you want to stay married for a long time, celebrate the good. And remember — it's *all* good.

Enrich Your Environment

There's yet another reason why we love to celebrate with our customers and with each other: it's fun! Sharing a meal together or racing go-carts or playing laser tag lets us see each other in a whole new light. I know of a company that took its customers to a huge indoor facility with climbing walls and zip lines and turned everyone loose. The customers had a blast watching the CEO being strapped into a harness and slid overhead on the zip line. It was a chance to let their hair down after several months of intense work and back and forth negotiations to get the job done just right. That level of intensity needs to be balanced with some form of relief, comic or otherwise.

We need that same balance to enrich and enliven our environment at home. The requisite tension that goes with managing work and a busy household can take its toll on any relationship. Every day, it seems, we need to make at least one important decision that affects our children, our finances, our friends, or our schedules. Charita and I are both usually running at top speed, doing our best to be good parents and supportive spouses, and if we're not careful, our game faces become permanent scowls. That's when I need to break the tension with a surprise trip to the ice cream shop or an impromptu back yard soccer game. Why? For the fun of it. To ensure that our home is not only a refuge but a playground, a place where laughter reigns and we see each other as our truest selves. In terms of balance, your kids see plenty of evidence that you're responsible and hardworking. They know you have a lot on your plate and have to do all the things grownups do, but too much emphasis on that can actually be harmful. A fascinating study of school-aged children during hard times found that financial woes often produced anxiety, depression, and behaviorial problems in kids. Those effects were significantly minimized in families that kept their focus on doing the things families usually do rather than continually focusing on problems.[12]

In other words, your kids need to see you in a party hat as often as they see you in a hard hat.

Forget Your Anniversary

When you think of celebrations in your family, you usually think of birthdays and anniversaries, with a couple of significant holidays like Christmas and the Fourth of July thrown in for good measure. Those are all great opportunities to celebrate, so I'm not really recommending you forget your wedding anniversary. Bad idea. But don't let those be your only occasions to celebrate. Most families miss the almost daily opportunities to turn everyone's attention toward what is good and honorable. If you need to jump-start your own list of reasons to celebrate in your family, consider these.

Good grades. Your kids work hard to turn in their assignments and memorize their times tables. When you see a smiley face or an A+ on one of their papers, throw an impromptu party, even if it's just a special mention at the dinner table.

No cavities. If the semiannual trip to the dentist offers proof that your kids really do brush their teeth regularly, make a big deal of it. You're rewarding good behavior and finding an excuse to have some fun.

Loser day. If Mom or Dad is on a diet and makes some progress, pour everyone a tall glass of water and hand them a carrot stick.

Firsts. First day of school. First Communion. First day of spring, summer, fall, and winter. First day of a new job. First snow. First bike ride without training wheels. First broken bone.

Big accomplishments. Charita runs marathons and triathlons. Making it to a finish line 26.2 miles away is a big deal and requires a big celebration. So do dance recitals, Little League championships, Olympics of the Mind awards, and so on.

Little accomplishments. Dad fixed the showerhead. Mom found her glasses. The kids finished a jigsaw puzzle. The dog learned a new trick. We made it to church on time.

The other anniversaries. Keep your family history alive by celebrating the day you moved into your present home, the day you proposed to your wife, the anniversary date for your job, the day you quit smoking, the day your parents or grandparents got married.

I'm not suggesting you make every day a big celebration. That diminishes the overall effect and eventually you have just a series of obligations that clutter up your lives. But if you don't find a way at least once a month to celebrate and reward yourselves with something fun that is tied to the good things about your family, you're depriving yourself and your family of the joy that comes with relationships.

One last note. This won't be easy for you. At work, I may be the one who suggests we need to do something special with a customer, but I get a lot of help in the execution. If my staff left it up to me to plan these events, our celebrations would be pretty dull. This is something you need to work together on with your wife. Commit together to enhance the climate in your home with some efforts to celebrate the good that happens regularly, to make the ordinary extraordinary.

Strong marriages and families don't just happen. They require diligence, dedication, and a fair amount of hard work. If in my business I expected everyone to keep their noses to the grindstone and never recognized their efforts, it would be an undesirable place to work. Our homes can similarly become overrun with tension and strife if we don't balance the hard work with some fun. The best way to do that is to celebrate your successes, and if you made it through the day and are sitting at the dinner table together, that's reason enough right there!

17

Building an Enduring Brand

I CAN'T SAY THAT I ENJOY ATTENDING FUNERALS, BUT I ALWAYS learn something from them. Such was the case with the funeral of a prominent Nashville businessman who had invested a lot of his time and energy into the city. The church where his funeral was held was packed with business leaders, politicians, the media, and other local celebrities, and it seemed as if most made their way to the platform to offer their tributes to this departed giant in our community. But as each speaker eloquently praised this man for his contributions to the city and its institutions, it struck me that not a word was said about him as a husband or father. He was lauded for being a successful businessman, for having a dynamic vision, for being innovative, and for giving back to the city that he loved so much. Yet nothing was said about his personal life. As I left the church, I was a bit shaken because I began to wonder what might be said at *my* funeral. Will I be known only as a successful businessman?

What I learned from that funeral is that someday I will be gone, and if all I leave behind is a business and some money, I will have failed as a man. The Bible exhorts us to invest in things that "moth and rust do not destroy," yet the world in which we live teaches us the opposite: make as much money as you can; give some away to get a building named after you. As I heard all those tributes for this man, I became determined to leave a different legacy, one that may not result in my name on a building but will live on in the lives of my children, and their children, and beyond.

In the business world, we call this branding—establishing and constantly working to develop a reputation that distinguishes your business from all of your competitors' businesses. Some companies have done this so well that their brand actually has become synonomous with the product: we reach for a Kleenex, even if the tissue is another brand; we used to Xerox things when we were actually just copying them; some people call any dark carbonated drink a Coke because they've established such a well-known brand. (Sorry, Pepsi.)

So what's *your* brand as a husband and dad? As a family?

I recently attended another funeral—one for my wife's great aunt—and this one only served to strengthen my resolve to invest in what really matters. This dear woman died in her eighties, leaving behind four generations of relatives who are a testament to her faith and integrity. She wasn't famous, but it was practically standing room only at her funeral. The service itself was a celebration of life rather than a parade of accomplishments. She was remembered as a godly wife and mother but also as someone who repeatedly found ways to help others along the way, who was honest to a fault, who sacrificed by putting the needs of her family ahead of her own. There were few tears and plenty of laughter as we celebrated a life well lived. Will we miss her? Absolutely, but as my wife said, "She will live forever *through* us." Talk about an enduring and respected brand.

After the funeral, some of the older relatives sat in a circle and sang her favorite hymns and told stories about her life. I felt as if I was on holy ground in the presence of these men and women in their eighties and nineties who have similarly built a brand that moth and rust cannot touch. This woman of God couldn't have left a better gift to my own children as they witnessed the fruits of a life celebrated rather than mourned.

We Carry Around What We Will Leave Behind

When I think of branding in business, I think of the great brands that have withstood the test of time, legacy brands that translated success in their particular sectors into local or national reputations. They were the names that people had grown up with, grown accustomed to, and knew what to expect from. International brands such as Mercedes, Nike, Sony, and Rolex are recognized around the world for their greatness, their commitment to excellence. And their reputation is passed on from generation to generation. Because the leaders of these companies paid attention to the right priorities, consumers from Cairo to Chicago know exactly what to expect when they buy a Rolex watch or a Mercedes automobile: they are getting the best.

Individuals leave legacy brands too. Your legacy brand is what you leave behind, what you are remembered for. When my in-laws and other relatives gathered to celebrate the passing of my wife's great aunt, they verbally passed around what she left behind: her generous spirit, her love for God, her devotion to her family. Had she left millions of dollars to her family, it wouldn't have come close to the value of her legacy, because no amount of money can buy you a reputation.

It's easy to think about these things at a funeral, but when we get back into the rhythms of life, the tyranny of the urgent often rules the day. But the convergence of these funerals with our efforts to draw up a will confronted me with the reality that someday I will be gone and that I don't want to leave behind just some money and a few possessions. I want to leave a legacy—an enduring brand recognition —and I think you do too. So how do we make sure we leave something behind that has lasting value?

Great branding doesn't happen overnight. Every now and then I hear someone declare he or she is starting a new tradition. I have to laugh to myself. Starting a tradition is easy; it's the keeping of it that gets in the way. A brand, like a tradition, takes time. What you are doing right now is determining your brand. Great brands are built on consistent, principled behavior. The values you embrace *today* become part of your brand. The way you face *today's* disappointment determines how you are remembered after you are gone.

The other day, my son, Caleb, said to me, "Dad, you know why people like you?" His question took me by surprise, and without thinking much about it I asked, "Why's that, Caleb?"

"It's because you open doors for people."

We were heading into a mall, and I never gave it any thought. I was just doing as I was taught and wasn't at all trying to be an example. It never even crossed my mind that opening a door for someone could have such an impact on my son. But it struck me: *he* noticed. Not only did he notice I opened a door for someone, he apparently is paying attention to whether others like me. Wow! Pretty daunting. But the people who love us the most *are* paying attention. They are watching us, not to catch us doing something wrong but to gain some clues as to how to live their own lives. The building of my brand with my wife began the day I met her; with my kids, the day they were born. It is a process, not a prescription.

Great brands require discipline. The great Yankees shortstop Alex Rodriguez was clearly on his way to the Baseball Hall of Fame. His admission that he used a banned performance-enhancing drug put all that in jeopardy. But whether or not this blot on an otherwise stellar career keeps him out of the hall, his brand has changed from superhero to cheater, all because of a momentary lapse of discipline. It could be said that all of the tarnished sports stars who have used steroids were highly disciplined athletes who didn't need drugs to perform well. But discipline isn't something you turn on and turn off.

You and I face temptations every day. It may not seem fair, but one moral or ethical mistake will erase the influence of all the times you exercised good discipline. Do you know your Achilles' heel? You should, because that's likely where you will be tempted the most. Don't let the good that you have done be clouded by an asterisk.

Your brand reveals your truest self. You can't fake a brand. A brand is not built on pretense. Like Caleb, your sons and daughters are paying attention. They know who you are. When Tim Russert, the legendary host of *Meet the Press*, died unexpectedly in the summer of 2008, tributes poured in from around the world. Fellow journalists, competitors, even guests who had been grilled by Russert all spoke of his integrity, his work ethic, his love for church and family. But what impressed me was that his son, Luke, affirmed those same qualities in his tribute. The elder Russert's colleagues saw him at work. His son saw him outside the glare of the cameras and in the privacy of their home, and he was the same guy.

Brands exist for others, not for you. Obviously, I want to leave a rich legacy, as do you. But in the end, it's not about us. We won't be around to enjoy it. What you invest in your brand is a deposit into the lives of others. Your brand won't be of much help to you, but it will provide inspiration and direction for others. It's not that you don't gain anything in the building of a great legacy: a life well lived and the knowledge that you will continue to shape others after you are gone. But if your primary motive for establishing a great brand is self-serving, it won't be much of a brand.

A eulogy is not a brand. Eulogies are great, and I hope a few people will say some nice things about me at my funeral. For that matter, there's nothing wrong with having a building named after you. It reminds people that you were successful *and* generous. But eulogies and the physical structures we leave behind are not brands. People are *expected* to say nice things about you at funerals. I've been to a few funerals where I had to check to make sure I was at the right place because all the nice things being said in the eulogy didn't quite track with what I knew about the deceased. We don't write brands; we live them.

A Life Worth Studying

Every issue of the *Harvard Business Review* includes at least one case study in which one of the editors creates a fictitious company facing a unique challenge, then invites business leaders to recommend how to solve it. Even though the companies are fictitious, you learn a lot about good business practices from the experts who study the company. I've always tried to run my business in such a way that if others studied it, they would learn something valuable that they could apply to their own businesses.

Many books have been written about the great legacy companies of our era. IBM and its historic turnaround. Microsoft's meteoric growth. GE and its ability to adapt to change. The bestselling book *Good to Great*, by Jim Collins, studies several successful companies to help others learn their secrets of success. Reading books like this inspires me to model my company after some of these companies that have built strong brands. I know my company may never be as big as GE, but I can learn from them and use what I learn to build a better company.

When I think of how I live my life and what I can leave for my loved ones, I realize that in a particular era, hundreds of millions of people will be born and die, but if you look at history, there are only a few hundred people whom we study, whom we look at and say, "That life was worth documenting; that life was worth looking into." My challenge to you: make your life worth studying. I have no aspirations of making history, but I do want to be someone my loved ones can study and use what they learn to be better people. I want my wife to be able to look up to me, just as I look up to her, and I want to be someone who inspires her to reach her own great potential. We try so hard to leave our mark at work—to be the top salesperson or lead the division in revenue growth. What if we were just as passionate about being such an impact player at home, to live a life worth studying so that we are a textbook of promise for the ones we love the most?

Dreams Die without Feet

I am convinced that most people of faith want to live the kinds of lives that create a legacy. We want to inspire our loved ones first, and then others, by our example. But like the legendary Walter Mitty in the James Thurber short story ("The Secret Life of Walter Mitty"), too many of us dream of a heroic life rather than live one. We wish our wives and children would look on us more favorably, but we lumber along doing the same things we've always done at home, expecting a different outcome. Dreams are good. They have the power to lift our hearts and inspire our minds, but without action, dreams die.

Take ownership of your dreams today and begin taking small steps to turn them into reality. If you desire to live a life of significance and you believe that requires a career change, do it! Sure it's risky, but what a great opportunity for your family to see a courageous husband and father invest in something so big that if he's successful, it could change the world. And if you fail, it does nothing to diminish the courage they will carry with them as part of your legacy.

If you want to be the father who shares a popsicle with his daughter on a hot summer afternoon and teaches her how to ride a two-wheeler, don't wait until "someday." Do it now. Carve out the time so that you can give yourself to her unrushed and unconcerned about anything but her. She will remember that far longer than she will remember your coming home all excited about a promotion.

If you want to be the husband whose wife can say at his funeral, "I have no regrets," take care of business today. If you spoke harshly to her this morning, call her right now and make it right. Commit today to treat her *better* than your best customer so that your son learns how to treat a woman and your daughter knows what to seek in a man. It doesn't matter if you're homeless or the ambassador to France, you can make changes in your life today to ensure a legacy that will inspire others to greatness.

Unfinished Business

I wrote this book because I believe marriage should be far more rewarding than it is for most people and that turning good marriages into great marriages is within our reach. I have seen too many men and women squander the skills that made them so successful at work by giving only their leftovers to the people who matter most in their lives.

But I also have seen what happens when people put as much effort into their families as they do their colleagues and customers, and it is amazing. Such as a sales executive who knows what wine to order when he hosts a key client, but also serenades his wife at night with "Be Thou My Vision" because he knows that's her favorite hymn. Is it any wonder she has such passion for him? And a CEO who personally inspects products before they are shipped to make sure they are just right, but who lost ten pounds in two months because he believes his wife deserves the best person he can be. And a technician who hops on a plane at moment's notice to repair a customer's network server, then takes the red-eye home so he can still drive his daughter to school. These guys aren't just being good husbands and dads; they're protecting their most important assets. They're investing in the very fabric of society, because research has shown that strong marriages and healthy families have a positive influence on communities. And they're building brands that will continue to influence others long after they are gone.

I want to be that kind of man. I want to be someone who is known more for his character than his accomplishments. And when they list my titles, I want husband and dad to be at the top of the list. I want my family to know that they are more important to me than any client or customer without my ever having to tell them, because they will see it.

I have great hope because I already know what to do. And so do you. We practice every day at work the skills that can make us heroes at home. Pleasing our customers, making them feel important, helping them to be successful — that's practically second nature to us. Now all we have to do is bring it home with us.

Which is what I had to do several years ago. I had to practice what I have been preaching.

Every morning before I leave the house for work, I say goodbye to everyone. Charita gets a hug and a kiss, and since I drive Caleb to school, he gets a little extra time. But my daughter, Zoé, has found a way to turn my farewell into about thirty to forty minutes of hugs and kisses and then some more hugs before I say a little prayer for her for that day. She just seems to need that extra time with her daddy, and of course I love it too. Every morning it's the same. As I'm waking up I hear her little feet coming down the stairs, and I know in a few seconds she'll be jumping into our bed for her special time.

I usually try to schedule my flights later in the morning so that as long as I'm in town I get to enjoy this little exercise with Zoé, but one day I had an early flight and needed to get going before anyone else was up. So I quietly got ready and as I opened the door to the garage, I heard those little feet of Zoé's. I knew if I went back in, I might miss my flight, and that would really mess things up for me that day. For a split second I thought about just hopping in the car and making a quick getaway and letting Charita handle things with Zoé, but then I set my bag down, turned around, and walked back into the house. By now, Zoé was crying uncontrollably, and when she saw me she just wailed, "Daddy, you didn't *bless* me today!"

It was then I realized that no flight, no meeting, and no customer is more important to me than my little Zoé. She was so used to my praying over her each day that she couldn't face the day without it. She didn't necessarily need the thirty minutes of hugging and cuddling, but she *did* need her daddy to bless her before he left. Which of course I did, and I still made my flight.

Guys, I know we're busy doing the right things. And I know it's not always easy. But in all of our busyness, let's never forget the privilege we have to bless our best customers. When you hear little feet coming after you, set everything down and receive those hugs from those who love you the most.

18

Imagine the Best

AT VARIOUS POINTS IN THIS BOOK, I HAVE ASKED YOU TO RECALL the earliest days of your relationship with your wife, to think back on how thrilling it was to fall in love with someone and have her return that love. I was appealing to your memory, and I can almost guarantee that those memories were wonderfully pleasant. Nothing quite matches the feeling of beginning a loving relationship that you intend to last a lifetime.

Now I would like to appeal to your imagination. How would your life be different if you reclaimed just 10 percent of that excitement for your marriage? How would your relationship with your wife be different if you spent only half as much time showing her you love her than you did when you first began dating? What would next Friday night be like if you planned an evening with her as thoughtfully as you did when she accepted that first date with you?

I know that you can't sustain "puppy love" forever, but I truly believe that we can expect much more from our marriages than many of us are getting. Yes, honeymoons must end, but that doesn't mean we can't still enjoy excitement, romance, tenderness, and fulfillment in our marriages. Regardless of the condition of your marriage, I

215

know it can become better by applying the very same principles and skills you use every day at work.

At first, it may seem a little overwhelming to transfer to your marriage all those skills that make you successful at work. How can you possibly do all these things? You probably can't, so I suggest you first sit down with your wife and invite her to join you in putting the principles of this book to work in your relationship. I don't know too many wives who would not be thrilled to learn that her husband wants to invest more of himself into their marriage.

Then go back through the chapters and select just one principle and make it a priority to apply it to your marriage for a week or so. For example, go back to the chapter on integrity ("Your Word Is Your Bond," page 97). Explain to your wife that you want to make sure she knows that she can trust you and that you want to show her that you are trustworthy by giving her access to all your personal accounts. Tell her you want to end each day with an accountability check and that you will let her know if you've even *thought* about keeping anything from her that day. Once you put into practice what you have learned in this chapter, select another one. And then another. Don't worry if it takes you several months to fully transfer what you have learned from work into your home life. I have read that it usually takes at least twenty-one days to develop a habit, so give yourself time to let these good habits take root.

Maybe this story from Dennis will encourage you. Dennis is one of those guys who prides himself on keeping his office neat and uncluttered. He was coached early in his career that the condition of his office is a reflection of his professionalism, so he always left time at the end of the day to clear off his desk and make sure everything was in its place. He had a couple of plants on a table by the window, and he even made sure they were watered every week. He just felt his clients would feel more confident (he's a financial advisor) if when they stopped in for an appointment, his office wasn't a study in chaos.

However, at home Dennis was something of a slob, which caused his wife considerable annoyance when the pile of clothes on the chair began to resemble a small mountain. It was never a huge deal, but it seemed that about once every few weeks she reached her limit, and then he would dutifully hang everything up or put it in the laundry. When he heard about the premise of this book, he saw an opportunity to practice at home what was second nature at work. He told his wife that he wanted to honor her as much as he did his clients and that he would take time every night to put his clothes where they belonged.

That lasted for about a week.

"Despite my good intentions, I once again had a pile of clothes on the chair and my wife just looked at me and smiled, almost as if to say, 'I knew it was too good to be true.' For some reason her response did the trick for me. I didn't want my clients to expect something from me that my own wife couldn't expect."

In other words, you probably won't bat a thousand on treating your wife as your customer, but hang in there. Don't let occasional setbacks discourage you.

When the Going Gets Tough

I don't know about your relationship with your wife, but sometimes just when things seem to be going great in our relationship, something comes up that creates tension between Charita and me. It's generally never a big fight or anything, but clearly we're hitting one of those rough spots that neither of us enjoy. I'm enough of a realist to know that every marriage — even the best of them — will have these occasional difficulties, but as I reflect on them I've come to see that they almost always happen when I let the demands of my job take precedence over my wife and family. All of my energy has been devoted to treating my customers like, well, customers. Fortunately,

I have a very understanding wife who gives me plenty of space when the stress builds at work, but I don't want to ever use that as an excuse for ignoring the needs of my family. I know you don't either, so here's a little secret that has helped me a lot: the returns on treating your wife and children as your customers are greatest when you do it during times when your work demands the most out of you. It's one thing to give your family great customer service when everything's going fine, but do it when you're putting in one of those monster sixty-hour weeks and you'll experience customer loyalty like you've never seen at work. Trust me, I know it's not easy, but you'll be glad you did it.

One final caution. Don't expect instant results. I'm convinced that if you treat your wife and children with the same level of respect and commitment that you give your customers, clients, and colleagues, you will enjoy a better relationship with them. But it may not happen overnight. I'm generalizing here, but guys tend to be results oriented. We think in terms of cause and effect. If I do x, then y will happen. Like the guy who finally learned to pick up his socks, you may need to establish a track record, and it's not your wife's fault if she takes a wait-and-see attitude. Too many times we make a little change in our behavior and then get upset when it isn't rewarded with lavish praise. Don't do any of the things I've described in this book in order to score points; do them because they will make you a better husband and father. Do them because it's right. At the end of the day, your wife doesn't want to see you jumping through hoops to please her. She just wants to be loved and valued, and your consistent—even imperfect—efforts to treat her like a customer will convice her she's both.

Pick up any book about starting your own business and at some point they will all say the same thing: being an entrepreneur is exciting and can produce tremendous satisfaction, but it is hard work. Really hard work. Most warn that if you're not willing to put in long hours and go through some very tough times, don't try it. The same could be said about marriage. It promises wonderful benefits, but they come only to those who are willing to do the work. Like most good things in life, a good marriage doesn't just happen; it requires two people who are fully engaged in the enterprise and are willing to invest their time and energy into their relationship.

So consider this an adventure, a journey that will lead you and your wife into a better, stronger, and more fulfilling marriage. Let her in on it from the beginning. Invite her to hold you accountable. Keep your sense of humor and be the first to admit it when you screw up. (Because you will!) And always remember: you got married because you didn't want to go through life alone.

If you've been feeling a little distant from your traveling companion, start treating her like your customer.

Notes

1. Marty Blalock, "Listen Up: Why Good Communication Is Good Business," *Wisconsin Business Alumni Update*, December 2005, *http://www.bus.wisc.edu/update/winter05/business_communication.asp*.

2. American Counseling Association, "Ten Steps for Improving Relationship Communications," *Counseling Corner*, July 21, 2008, *http://www.counseling.org/Publications/CounselingCorner.aspx?AGuid-5f4fafc2-3822-4348-8eaa-8e341a6 72129*.

3. Daniel Kadlec, "The Prenup Audit," *Time*, June 28, 1999, *http://www.time.com/time/magazine/article/0,9171,991358,00.html*.

4. G. Jeffrey MacDonald, "Lying," *Christian Science Monitor*, June 23, 2004, *http://www.csmonitor.com/2004/0623/p15s01-lire.html*.

5. Teresa Turner Vining, "Drifting Apart," *Focus on the Family*, June 2008, *http://www2.focusonthefamily.com/focusmagazine/marriage/A000001129.cfm*.

6. Louis McBurney, "Are You Drifting Apart?" *Marriage Works Magazine*, October 2007, *http://www.mwmagazine.com.au/?p=210http://www.mwmagazine.com.au/?p=210*.

7. Jane Weaver, "Many Cheat for a Thrill, More Stay True for Love," *MSNBC.com*, April 16, 2007, *http://www.msnbc.msn.com/id/17951664/*.

8. Judith Wallerstein, "The Long-Term Effects of Divorce on Children: A Review," *Journal of the American Academy of Child and Adolescent Psychiatry*, May 1991, 352.

9. Center for Marriages and Families at the Institute for American Values, "Does Divorce Make People Happy? Findings from a Study of Unhappy Marriages," June 2002, *http://center.americanvalues.org/?p=14*.

10. Mayo Clinic Staff, "Social Support: Tap This Tool to Reduce Stress," *http://mayoclinic.com/health/social-support/SR00033*.

11. Carol Mithers, "Faith in Marriage," *Ladies' Home Journal*, *http://www.lhj.com/relationships/divorce/communication/faith-in-marriage/*.

12. Sue Shellenbarger, "When Tough Times Weigh on the Kids," *Wall Street Journal*, September 24, 2007, *http://online.wsj.com/article/SB122220949327768879.html*.

Share Your Thoughts

With the Author: Your comments will be forwarded to the author when you send them to *zauthor@zondervan.com*.

With Zondervan: Submit your review of this book by writing to *zreview@zondervan.com*.

Free Online Resources at
www.zondervan.com

Zondervan AuthorTracker: Be notified whenever your favorite authors publish new books, go on tour, or post an update about what's happening in their lives at www.zondervan.com/authortracker.

Daily Bible Verses and Devotions: Enrich your life with daily Bible verses or devotions that help you start every morning focused on God. Visit www.zondervan.com/newsletters.

Free Email Publications: Sign up for newsletters on Christian living, academic resources, church ministry, fiction, children's resources, and more. Visit www.zondervan.com/newsletters.

Zondervan Bible Search: Find and compare Bible passages in a variety of translations at www.zondervanbiblesearch.com.

Other Benefits: Register yourself to receive online benefits like coupons and special offers, or to participate in research.

We invite you to continue your experience with *Treat Me Like a Customer* at *www.louisupkins.com*:

- Share how you feel about *Treat Me Like a Customer* and read what others are saying.
- Share your insights and discuss the book with other readers at the *Treat Me Like a Customer* forum.
- Communicate with the author.

If you enjoyed *Treat Me Like A Customer*, please consider these ideas for passing it on:

- Buy ten copies and give them to people you think this book will help.
- Use this book as a gift for your employees or customers.
- Create small groups to discuss how you can start treating your family like a customer.
- Share it with your friends on Facebook, MySpace, and Twitter.

For information about having the author speak to your organization or group, please visit *www.louisupkins.com*.